POLEMICS

POLEMIcS

Anselm Hollo   Anne Waldman
Jack Collom

Autonomedia

Dedicated to the Memory of Allen Ginsberg,
dear Naropa colleague and friend

"Candor ends Paranoia."

Some of the enclosed pieces by Anne Waldman have appeared in the following places: The Shambhala Sun, The Poetry Project Newsletter, Bombay Gin, Napalm Health Spa, *Iovis II* (Coffee House Press), Pasta Poetics, intent, Anatomy: Raw, Woodstock Review, *American Poets Say Goodbye to the 20th Century* (Four Walls Eight Windows). The author also cites and thanks the following writers for lines of inspiration in "Kali Yuga Poetics" and other texts: William S. Burroughs, Subcomandante Marcos, Vaclav Havel, Edward Said, Hakim Bey, H.D., William Blake, Robert Duncan, Beverly Dahlen, Pam Rehm, Bernadette Mayer, Joseph Ceravolo, Nathaniel Mackey, Noam Chomsky, Frank O'Hara.

Some of the enclosed pieces by Jack Collom have appeared in the following places: *Arguing With Something Plato Said* (Rocky Ledge Editions), Exquisite Corpse, Bombay Gin, The Mouse Poems, The New Amazing Grace, Alternative Press postcards, Gate (Germany), Napalm Health Spa, Anatomy: Raw, Broken Rock/Empty Water, In This Corner, Ecompost, *The Task* (Baksun Books), *Entering The City* (The Backwaters Press), Talisman, *American Poets Say Goodbye to the 20th Century* (Four Walls Eight Windows).

ISBN# 1-57027-070-8

Autonomedia
PO Box 568, Williamsburgh Station
Brooklyn, NY 11211-0568
autonobook@aol.com
www.autonomedia.org
this book printed in the United States of America

Authors' Note: It was the interesting idea of Peter Lamborn Wilson to have a little politico-polemico anthology from The Jack Kerouac School of Disembodied Poetics at the Naropa Institute. We three have been colleagues a good number of years in this fertile and interactive context as poets, teachers, performers, thinkers, humans. Here is an offering — a combination that gives a taste of our distinct yet complementary poetries and daily politics. As we go to press, our school moves into its 25th year of the planet. The planet moves into...?

—Anselm Hollo, Anne Waldman, Jack Collom
January 1998, Boulder, Colorado

CONTENTS

Part I

Anselm Hollo

Fool's Paradise

"You
live in a Fool's Paradise..."

"Yes!   It's *home!*"

Cells grow tree
& in it,
heavy cicadas

They finite
We gone

Stop, dear Mozart:
You're making me cry

Sure *I* killed a bunch of Chinese—
they're *tall*—
them Veetnamese are *small*—"

handsome man in his thirties
clean & with it   pickin' up a sixpack

looks perfectly capable

but is given to these fits of weeping

Ginkgo tree
was here
before dinosaurs

Sometimes I feel like an idiot boychild
longing for Mama Ocean

Oh would you ride with the religious?

Oh no I'm just an old crank

Now that the old confusions
have been moved out & junked
the heart looks rather empty

"Boy   you gotta carry that weight"
I remember it well   that song

& mushrooms have been here all along

Watch it   go by
"Oil Is an Act of God"   "Come Home to America"

"You always laughed at those things
It took a little time   but you laughed"

Someone in movie   some remarkable dreck
I step into, slip

"You've sublimated that into 'oops-a-daisy'"

Dreaming, deprogramming, then awake
convulsed with rage-mirth at suave golem-blather
chewed ends of blond-gray Fu Manchu
grown out of middle-aged stoned chin

Object speaks
Object has spoken

in irritable parentheses

Seen the Divine
Seen the Chorizo
Seen the Radio
Heard it too

Smash bad faith (pretense) says the feathered speaker
sweet shoes goofy grace & heartbreak kid
what happened to us Fred   my little arm hurts
in the great Dracula organ roar of existence

Queen Anne's Lace out my window, Virginia

I don't have to go to the bloody store every day

But where else *is* there to go in this bloody place
or any other place in this bloody society
this bloody monolith of "store"

& when I say bloody I mean bloody   like Joseph Spero
mob store operator in Kansas City
"accidentally exploded" a while ago

"After all, the old bum is your father"
as Buster Keaton pointed out a while ago

In the great return engagements
between the nineteenth & twentieth centuries
we'll experience many surprises

As for the news, it's still punched in & out
by obedient punks   I know, I was one
for almost a decade

Until one day on a very ordinary bus
suddenly deprived of impressions   I became aware
once more   of the painful & weary
& tired of all sensational beauty tips tricks & freebies

It was the time of early to mid-period Rolling Stones
their diction was excellent then   it was a help
as was Herbert Marcuse

There's this Assyrian rite
survives in southern Italy:

a year after death,
you dig up bones

& take them home,
& polish them, & talk to them:

"Dear Aunt Maria,
dear Uncle Gesualdo" et cetera

All night, all day,
you polish them, talk to them,

then put them back,
in the ground.

Buenas días, Argentina.
Buenas días, Cambodia.

Buenas días, Russia,
Buenas días, America.

Stars   stars   all around

The air-borne laser lab

       new god of all good Soviets
                     good Americans

Some of them some of us positive roses

Like those blooming in wild Russian jungle garden
around this house now

There's obvious love in some houses

But Queen Anne's Lace no way out cowboy hats no way out

It's time time again to come out of the cave

(& go to the store)

After Wang Wei to be sure this is a frail old house
but sturdy table
writing hand bandaged but functional
wine by my elbow
the lady beautiful wise & forbearing
beyond my deserts (1)
beyond my deserts (2)

James Dean
now dead
as long as he was alive
to himself

An amusing distinction

"So you really want to know how it is with me?"
as some poet might say in that strange place
known as translation
in muffled gutturals one strains to hear
the other side of massive airlock glass

Well everything's pretty great really
but for poverty illness mortality   & so on

Language it   think   think big
big sentence

Then let no more remain
than of Doc Hipponax

                Doc Hipponax

                Hip Dog

We tend to think the world sort of stands up
while all it really does is roll around

Women's laughter through crickets & tree frogs

Hum hum twilight's
Halloween, year's
dusk   every day   Diodoros
of Aspendos

redeems the vulture cultures

Sleazeville Collegeville Pentagon

hospital follies   a long cold drive

& bathroom mirror says:
"old man, some bloody *sense*"

(remember the Professor
whose name translates as Garbage?)

Diodoros   two teeth left, barefoot, grinning
"broad beans? sure, I'll have some"
with the blue eyes of a bay scallop
at his best when alone & confused   at large

Hum hum   "you gotta *serve* somebody"
Ah, the new self-righteous righteousness:

"They behaved like sickening pigs"
What a way to speak of your elders

But when the new self-righteous righteous
speakers & singers look up
they see their "Lord"

When they look down
they see shit on their shoes

"What a self-indulgent jackoff!"
I hear you say

but I do not understand those phonemes

Because I am Diodoros
of Aspendos   Pythagorean
of the last days   disguised as a Cynic

I want to thank my mother
my family
my lawyers

& here they come

congaing through my pillow

just like "god"

this faded purple box of five thousand
"Standard Swingline Staples Number S.F. Minus One"
has lasted me through
a marriage or two
almost a dozen addresses phone numbers
defunct checking accounts
seven years & some months
& I still have a couple of hundred left

As for belief only one thing to believe
when she or he love you they do   but what do it mean
Ah amigo that's the trick   funny voices in corners
of room-shaped head I'm sorry I got a deadline will you
come back later oil is an act of god

How to get back to conscientious Francis Scott Fitzgerald
or ancestor who ate a cat's heart   It is four a.m. back on
schedule   more words per square centimeter
conventional even sentimental historical
late mechanized heir to romance

Then somewhat speculative & fictional some what
misheard with inner & outer in other words actual by another
not unlike constructive analogous & inconclusive yet mostly
attempts & mentioned synchronous subsequent & compositional
having always held tuning-in possibly acquiring ability

To project voices out there in here & glad to be saying
hasta luego to do without knowing them again
Remember my little granite pail   Sat up all night roaring
overloaded most of the time   Who is this thinks
Point now not to country regional hopeless but theoretically

Sunlight falling on ten per cent United States farm land
supplies total Mehitabel joy some ways Lord Byron
some ways the incredibly blue eyes of a bay scallop
both see through the blob in age of inanition
apple crate art   great difficulties of honesty

Some remarkable dreck much of it sublimated into oops-a-daisy
dreaming deprogramming surviving Three Mile Island coming up
When you swim under water this is where you keep your lighter
Taps back pocket   John Sjoberg   Suppose I give you a pill
which makes you draw a picture   or one which gives you

Feelings in the stomach   This has been god's minute
The voice is calling & we are lonely for it   In esoteric
lore the lady is the least essential   No kidding   & whose
fault was it pardon me sir whose fault was it yours or hers
Common as hell put some heat on it get your ass up here

Uprose with hastie joy & feeble speed that agéd Sire
the Lord of all that land Yes well may you stay forever
incredible but know your underwear as it goes through the mangle
combine bottle brush trees with Rosa Luxemburg's prism &
your own paludal prurience   itspeak kitspeak

(signed) Otto & Myrtle Ampersand

Max Jacob: a moment's thought to
Max Jacob

Just a little artist
caught in the roiling of time hands grabbed him out of—

believed in weeding, they did,
& he was a weed

flowered beyond & above
the greatest French garden

was plucked & destroyed by those hands in black gloves:
regulation S.S., acronym for Schutzstaffel

"Protective Squadron"   Protective of what?
Of another little artist, a weed
grew like killer kudzu all over Europe

Was burned off her face
not much later:

Both their seeds
still circling the planet

Pissing on open grave of last morning's mouse
trapped in the house

Three a.m. Sweet Briar Virginia

Quiet   Madness   Insomnia   Tequila

Old Charles Laughton horror movie "Strange Door"

Dust whale vacuum cleaner in corner & now
it's one hundred degrees & I understand nothing
though still attentive just like the cat

to grotesque collective manifestation of regression:
some doddering lopsided smiler
our future leader?
Pea-brained predatory type
repeated
several thousand times   gleeful   jumping
up, down   blowing whistles   punching
little balloons in the air

back pockets stuffed with truly oily bills

Mad baby grins   bubbling   manic brain soup

"America   Behave   Or Be Damned"

That's Baptist billboard

You take deep breath   & drive on by

Totally wholly welcome is hokum
but it's nice hokum

People do think of people not here
& sometimes even hear them

Many years later there's a pleasant evening
with Mr. & Mrs. Hokum

& maybe Mrs. Hokum says, on parting:
"We *were*

a little worried about you
back there   for a while"

Sure been nice to meet all you people
the complicated simple
the simple complicated
the complicated complicated
the simple simple

Not as exciting as it was for your ancestors
or was it   confronting Red Cloud's negotiators

Just like you, like them, I've come to the end of the push:
the Beach Boys' concert

Finn Swede German Pole
& various smaller fractions Anglo Dutch & Martian
citoyen du monde

by the light of your campfires
                    shopping malls
                    museums
                    & a few good bars

No way to go now but out

                Let's figure it out

"Right side of face hurts more than the left"
Another pointless statement

Thousands upon thousands of those
made in this life   until it is over

Music fades in & out

Beat stays the same

Now "le beau reste"
as our French sisters say   *ah oui*
where do we go from here

round the page

We'll just go gamboling round the page
once again

& then

let's kill

all the bad guys

let's have

all the good guys

over for dinner

"What's for dinner?"

"Bad guys"

1979
revised 1995

NOTES

Fool's Paradise, originally titled *Frail Old House in Sweet Briar Patch,* was written in 1979 during a two-year stint as poet in residence at a small private college in Virginia, and published in my book *No Complaints* (West Branch, Iowa: The Toothpaste Press, 1983). Sixteen years later, it seemed to call for a few revisions, but its general tenor of response to local and global politics—compounded of disbelief, laughter, resignation, and rage—feels as appropriate as it did back then. In its *cento* passages, the poem incorporates brief quotes from movies, television, radio, Walter Benjamin, Bob Dylan, Robert Grenier, Don Marquis, Laurie McElroy, Lorine Niedecker, James Schuyler, John Sjoberg, Sir Edmund Spenser, Ludwig Wittgenstein, and probably others.

"Just think" and "Sure—*I* killed a bunch": Overheard snippets of conversation at the grocery store.

"As for the news, it's still punched in & out": Reference to the scribe's employment by a major Western European broadcasting corporation in the late Fifties/early Sixties.

"(remember the Professor/whose name translates as Garbage?)": The immortal protagonist of Henrich Mann's novel *Professor Unrat,* played by Emil Jannings in *The Blue Angel,* the movie based on that novel, which also featured the young Marlene Dietrich.

"Diodoros/of Aspendos": One of the few survivors (who often masqueraded as Cynics) of the anti-Pythagorean purges in the sixth century BCE. The Pythagoreans took part in politics, and their opposition to accepted religion caused them to be persecuted from existence in Magna Graecia. "broad beans? sure, I'll have some": Orthodox followers of Pythagoras never partook of beans.

Part II

Anne Waldman

Kali Yuga Poetics

for Hakim Bey

a practical jungle passed along through. nannies all of us looking for some haven that might have survived the holocause or hollow cast as the case may be some evil old bitch at least in a kiosk spitting drag but by the time we get there she is Sweet Old Flower Lady—

   —William S. Burroughs, *The Ticket That Exploded*

One hunts in other languages, cultures and cosmologies for a key or "code" to help interpret, penetrate, comprehend the destruction and the excision one experiences in the world. I hunt inside poetry. I want to unlock the secret syllables or runes that keep me a prisoner inside ignorance, confusion, thwarted awareness and desire. I want to sing and dance on the textcorpses of my ancestors and revel in the delight & soma-word soma/magic that antecedes my own and that of my generation—a sorcery that allows those bard-warriors, those faceless ones to rise when they need to out of their ashes. It's a call to ancient original alignments, intricate armaments of graceful & explicit language, dizzying beauties of syncretic communication that ruminate, articulate & vocalize continuously in the Kali Yuga voidzone. No one asks you to do this. The world-hallucination does not require it. Prayer & rant, mantra & pun & all slant of tongue, harangue & litany, communiques from various activity fronts enter in. Alternatives of all kinds that asked to happen by themselves. Arose out of unoriginated need. Unrequired. But a matter of life and death. Survival?

Kali Yuga Poetics is never out of date. It is self-existent. No one asks you to do this. *You do it*.

Kali Yuga Poetics intuits cognizance of this world-destruction, names it, transmutes it, literally deconstructs it, if only briefly for one sacramental poem, fragment of a holy song, to laugh at its folly, see ironies it holds, unfold how idiotic we've been, fix the abomination in imagination so as to comprehend it better, come into focus on a screen perhaps, call it up, fish it out of Indra's magnificent scintillating shimmering diamond net of inter-connected, inter-related energies. Indra—cosmological Lord of Universe type, thunder/rain god who keeps a fascinating web-work spinning constantly. *Pratitya-Samutpada*, Buddhist term for the co-originating interdependent interconnectedness of all living consciousness, sentience. Which too, can be, does not have to be, the endless spin of *Samsara*—the vicious cycles of transmigratory suffering. *Samsara* arises out of ignorance and is characterized by suffering. This is the mood of the Kali Yuga, a time frame. Is it familiar? Comfortable? Stuffy? Kali Yuga Poetics invites you in. No one asks you to do this, to go in—you have no choice.

The faceless ones continued speaking:

The world is another world, reason no longer governs and we true men and women are few and forgotten and death walks upon us, we are despised, we are small, our word is muffled, silence has inhabited our houses for a long time, the time has come to speak for our hearts, for the hearts of others, from the night and from the earth our dead should come, the faceless ones, those who are jungle, who dress with war so their voice will be heard, that their word later falls silent and they return once again to the night and to the earth, that other men and women may speak, who walk other lands, whose words carry the truth, who do not become lost in lies.

"Look for the men and women who lead obeying, those who have strength in their words, and not in fire, and finding them, speak and give them the staff of command, that they may return once again to the earth and the night, the faceless ones, those who are jungle, so that if reason returns to these lands the fury *of the fire may be silenced, that the faceless ones, those who go by night may rest at last by the earth."*

Thus spoke the faceless ones, there was no fire in their hands and their word was clear and without folds. And before the day defeated the night once again they went, and on the earth one word remained: "Enough!"

—Published in *La Jornada*, February 27, 1994.
   Translated by R. Nigh.
   (communique from the Zapatista Liberation Army)

Activity—or *karma* in Sanskrit—is a principle. Speech—*Vac*—is a given. By all accounts Speech—*Vac*—is a goddess. By that I mean you can get powerful urges around her. *Tantra*, in Sanskrit means thread or continuity. So a language I find useful is a language of Speech, Activity, Continuity. *Vac, Karma, Tantra*. And the atmosphere we are breathing which is *Kali Yuga*.

So we are given to speech and some of us call ourselves "writers," "poets." Complex syntactical and semantic structures inform our activity/art. What is the activity? What is an act of poetry? How does it differ from an act of aggression? If I do this to this this happens or that to that that happens or this to you this happens in you, to you and you do this to this to this to that to make that happen or make that happen in me to me and others and that hap-

47

pens back to you, always shifting never the same, back to you. Comes back to you at you. This to this to this to this to that to that to that. Dissipative structures eating entropy, strange attractors, modal structures, unnatural symmetries, unnatural realignments. Making gestures into a void. How long is the effect of a poem-gesture? Mirrors upon mirrors worlds upon worlds talking, fucking, dying. This to this to this. Rage upon rage. Violence upon violence, talking fucking dying. One small tune, a sung-fragment, a whispered wisp of poem-line:

Pompeii has nothing to teach us,
we know crack of volcanic fissure,
slow flow of terrible lava,

pressure on heart, lungs, the brain
about to burst its brittle case
(what the skull can endure!):

over us, Apocryphal fire,
under us, the earth sway, dip of floor,
slope of a pavement

where men roll, drunk
with a new bewilderment,
sorcery, bedevilment:

the bone frame was made for
no such shock knit within terror,
yet the skeleton stood up to it:

the flesh? it was melted away,
the heart burnt out, dead ember,
tendons, muscles shattered, outer husk dismembered,

yet the frame held:
we passed the flame: we wonder
what saved us? What for?
        —H.D., *The Walls Do Not Fall*

These lines conjured from a series of experiments ground-
ed in H.D.'s actual experience of the bombing of London
during WW II.

The president turns in his sleep and into his stupidity
        seep the images of
                burning peoples.
The poet turns in his sleep,   the cries of the tortured
        and of those whose pain

survives after the burning   survive with him,   for
        continually
he returns to early dreams of just retributions and
        reprisals inflicted for his injuries.
The soldier gloating over and blighted by the burning
        bodies of children,
                women and old men,
        turns in his sleep of Viet Nam or,
dreamless, inert, having done only his duty hangs at the
edge of such a conscience to sleep.

        —from Robert Duncan's *Groundwork I: Before The War*

"Cold, cold. Smoked the bitch" an American pilot said
bombing an Iraqi warplane. Indra's Net of unspeakable
deeds. Net of many tongues. The tongue of poetry being
one of them. We have not even described let alone been
able to conceptualize this virtual Gulf War yet. Several

hundreds of thousands of people were sacrificed for a scenario, a showcase of *things to come*. We got to show off & demonstrate our latest tactical weaponry. Karma of Vietnam vet Timothy McVeigh. The USA has over 20,000 nuclear weapons today with at least 10,000 of these being long-range strategic weapons designed for maximum accuracy and destructiveness. 3,500 produced after the Gulf War. The USA is the chief broker for this brave new industry. The W-61 Interim Earth Penetrator Warhead has been developed to target underground command posts and shelters for political and military leaders.

In 1492 when the Conquest began there existed about 320 languages in North America, these are down to about 100 in Native American languages. The amount of time it will take this planet to restore itself is immense. Who can ever restore these languages? Will multiple poetries replace these languages? What does one writer do? What language will be inhabited then? A tongue of poetry? You do this to this this happens. But the tenderer side too, bend down to kiss the child's milky brow, small teen sleeping so gently now. He stirs a little in sleep, warmly to be touched. Not sentimental talk about war, nobility, the cutting of deals. The Dept. of Energy says today Rocky Flats will take at least 70 years to make safe and cost 22 billion dollars, this sweet son an old man by then. And what of the landscape? *Someone must live to describe it in poetry*. New vocabularies, new tongues to describe an increasingly strange-seeming future. Seeming, the root of *samsara*, the world of appearance. From some point of view all those languages still exist, recorded in other interstices of time & place. Kali Yuga Poetics describes more than one universe.

As a description from numerous cosmologies with resonant sensibilities—Tibetan, Maya, Navaho—Kali Yuga literally refers to the current "dark age" mortals and everything else that breathes in ecological system H_2O earth-planet find themselves stuck in. This fishbowl-planet. From some point of view we are now more than ever before inhabiting a classically described hell-realm where not only the physical pressures are extreme, but the psychological ones as well. The amount of pain we have inflicted on ourselves on other beings on Nature is unspeakably intense. You could almost say infinite. Ecologist friend Peter Warshall reports there are 100 species a day dying on this planet, most of whom have no recorded names.We have not even taken the time to know and name what we kill. The planet itself has AIDS. The suffering experienced world wide at this moment at any fraction of a moment— as we speak now as I utter the word "now"—on this planet is inexorable, excruciating. The amount of suffering inflicted on children alone is unspeakable. Can one write or commit any creative act after Auschwitz it was asked? How long ago that seems. After Bosnia after Rwanda after East Timor after Afghanistan after Guatemala after Chernobyl after inner city America after countless other insanities, violent acts, bombings, genocides you'd have to ask again, again, again. But we have recognized this. Why harp on it, why not join the dance of skeletons nihilistically to the grave. It is amazing that we are not all completely out of our minds with grief. It is amazing that we can still have some semblance of holding it together. Yes one can write, commit a creative act after atrocities. We have to hold our poetry front. A self-fulfilling prophecy we all recognize, lying in the bed we most carelessly made, a kind of shallow grave. Inside it we scribble. Yet at the core of this planet is perhaps a giant crystal made of iron, The

New York Times proclaimed recently. This imagined is a poetry. Kali Yuga Poetics seizes on such images to keep spinning its wheel of compassion & suffering.

Blake's virgin Thel, the unborn peeks into what we call this life. This passage is Kali Yuga's anthem:

The eternal gates terrific porter lifted the northern bar:
Thel enter'd in & saw the secrets of the land unknown;
She saw the couches of the dead, & where the fibrous roots
Of every heart on earth infixes deep its restless twists:
A land of sorrows & of tears where never smile was seen.

She wandered in the land of clouds thro' valleys dark, listning
Dolours & lamentations: waiting oft beside a dewy grave
She stood in silence. listning to the voices of the ground,
Till her own grave plot she came, & there she sat down.
And heard the voices of sorrow breathed from the hollow pit.

Why cannot the Ear be closed to its own destruction?
Or the glistning Eye to the poison of a smile!
Why are Eyelids stord with arrows ready drawn,
Where a thousand fighting men in ambush lie?
Or an Eye of gifts & graces, show'ring fruits & coineds
gold! Why a Tongue impress'd with honey from every wind?
Why an Ear, a whirlpool fierce to draw creations in?
Why a Nostril wide inhaling terror trembling & afright?

Why a tender curb upon the youthful burning boy?
Why a little curtain of flesh on the bed of our desire?

The virgin started from her seat, & with a shriek.
Fled back unhinderd till she came into the vales of Har.

—William Blake, *The Book of Thel* (1789)

Kali Yuga Poetics is born of this prison sentence. Kali Yuga seizes Thel by the hand and pushes her into birth. Kali Yuga Poetics takes glee in its born-ness. She's Thel's promiscuous mother, this dread god Kali.

The words "Kali Yuga" insert themselves more deeply into my psycho-physical being:

A term from the Sanskrit Hindu cosmological system, *kali* from *kala* means black, or *the black of an eye.* More tangibly, *kali* is a type of resin, associated with the planet Saturn. *Kali* means, too, the worst of anything—"strife" or "quarrel." *Kal* carries the sense "to calculate or enumerate a fixed point of time." More dramatically, *Kali* refers to the terrifying Hindu destroyer Mother Goddess, one of the aspects of Durga (four-armed with weapons, dancing on dead Shiva, necklace of skulls or severed head, tongue dripping blood) who takes all composite beings & things & mental emotional states into her giant bloody maw, and spits the refuse out, unflinchingly.

I visited the Kalighat temple in Calcutta not too long ago from whence Calcutta gets her name. Devotees out of their minds with frenzied adoration jammed the trail hungry to get a glimpse of her frightful visage, swooning at the sight. The priests within the inner sanctum tend her like a doll. Wash her down, dress & paint her up, adorn her with ornaments. She's a poetical fetish, microcosm of the the Universe. Her mantras, songs on all worshippers' tongues.

According to legend, when Shiva's wife's corpse was cut up, one of her fingers fell at this place. Thus the thousands flock to the temple every day for a recharge of that

Kali Yuga Poetics does not bend to commerce or fold under spectres/images of current horrific events meant to intimidate, scare you off or numb your already stretched heart. But Kali Yuga Poetics is no salvation either. Kali Yuga Poetics visualizes real people in real situations and attempts contact through direct experience, words, exchanges of poetry, publications—'zines, articles, magazines, other resources—and through intelligent descriptive investigative writing. Kali Yuga projects cheerfulness, comraderie, gentleness, kindness, not idiot compassion, community spirit, exchanges of earth & sky, activism on many fronts. Kali Yuga Poetics sends writers armed with pens & pads & postcards & libraries into schools, prisons, homeless shelters, alternative radio & TV stations, print shops, and the public demonstration zone. It encourages volunteerism, going the extra exhausting mile. Kali Yuga Poetics suggests a poet have many skills. Kali Yuga Poetics views the Net as a powerful resource.

& these lines are chanted:

May the Net's byways and pathways always be kept free & open, not clogged with merchandise & sick & violent political agendas. May what is only a tool & we keep that perspective be a bastion against the anti-democratic Christian right and keep lines from Chiapas freedom fighters open, a few examples...

Kali Yuga Poetics recognizes these statistics:

That twice as many whites as either blacks or Latinos have home computers. That students from poor and minority families generally attend poorer public schools, where they are lucky if they have any exposure to computers, much less modems, the Net or any other frills.

Kali Yuga Poetics understands that technology is yet again another force, another demon that is widening the painful social and economic divide that already exists in American society, not to mention the rest of the world. That the very fabric of our society is ripped and broken by this increasing tear. This techno-rip. A tear. Even Hollywood cashes in on the painful reality. (See "Johnny Mnemonic" based on cyberspace-coiner William Gibson where the world is split into two classes: High Teks & Lo Teks.)

Kali Yuga Poetics is not naive. Kali Yuga Poetics does not spit upon or deride religion or spirituality although it mocks those who try to manipulate banner of god & country to their own devious purpose to limit freedoms of individuals, animals, planets, eco-systems on this planet. Kali Yuga Poetics hates gender problems. Kali Yuga Poetics is by turns amused & appalled by the mainstream. Its scared impotent sentimentality. Lost in hallucinations of toys & escape. Bad movies. Bad television. Kali Yuga Poetics boycotts commercial TV. Kali Yuga Poetics is in solidarity with all oppressed peoples, whether they know they are oppressed or not, although Kali Yuga Poetics does not mean to sound condescending. Kali Yuga Poetics studies war through old movies, books, father-in-laws, grandmothers & grandfathers. Kali Yuga Poetics talked hours to Jiri's mother in Prague who had survived many wars. "Aggression, coercion, it's all the same...whatever the agenda..." Kali Yuga Poetics casts no blames, or drives all blame into itself for positing such a difficult alternative to aggression & ignorance. You want to settle some scores? Kali Yuga Poetics tests its adherents to keep a sense of humor and rebound each day. Kali Yuga Poetics is not shocked by self-fulling prophecy. It sees the writing on the wall. Kali Yuga Poetics first saw evidences of terrorism in Beirut in the Sixties. Kali Yuga Poetics had a machine gun pointed to her head. Kali Yuga Poetics is not knowing it all but is not shocked either by the vicissitudes of outrageous karma and willpower. Kali Yuga's willpower is ultimately stronger. Kali Yuga Poetics is au courant & has views on everything, from baseball—those fuckers, both sides—to the commodification of the Beat Generation. Read more books. Kali Yuga Poetics is warm & holy. Kali Yuga Poetics makes no claims for enlightenment but has a better time. Kali Yuga Poetics devours & spits out then eschews critical theory. You play the gamelan to understand regenerative time cycles. Kali Yuga Poetics parts the curtain on duplicity. Kali Yuga Poetics grieves the many deaths and illnesses of friends. Kali Yuga Poetics practices meditation to make people well. Kali Yuga Poetics looks into the issue of assisted suicide for terminal AIDS & cancer patients meeting with an Ethics committee that worries the question for months in the state of Colorado. It's a personal issue, a decision that arises in the age of Kali Yuga. Kali Yuga Poetics finds abortion to be a painful experience. You think it's easy? But it's *my* body. The government does not own my body. Kali Yuga Poetics sees Rocky Flats disempowered plutonium factory as a conundrum for a quarter of a million years. Poetry keeps the heart safe. It keeps you on your toes to memorize a few lines. And it's not as if poetry can ward off old age sickness death don't be silly but it eases suffering. I'll say it again "Poetry eases suffering."

did you and away. our morning. our grief. our distraction. she garnished the wood.

a moment a rock at the bottom of a dry creek walking she bends and pockets it. a lost touch. in the story one longed to know the clean taste of fresh cucumber. a hill of daisies half blasted.one side blooms, one side goes on living.

there it was so we might discover the record of the pianist anyway. what had been his background. what, not dead yet. still some life there, some wanting to go on. those willfully cruel, those texts we cannot abide. what comes next. where is it.

half blasted wasted a hill, the flowering of the rod. these starknesses.

a new book, a new book, a book of torture. torture entered the everyday vocabulary of the newspapers. entered there. in. stayed there. we looked back on a time of torture.

wary with animals in an easy spring
the ghost of what's said
hounds on
weary with what's said
that broken skull hounds on
that tooth and nail bloody in
red in claw in fin
how small the while this looking
back to see it end

...

bide the time. it will hold you up. how we must deal with the unhappiness of other people.

    —Beverly Dahlen, *A Reading* (11-17)

Poetry is sanctuary of love, abandon, dance, vibration of the ancestors. Kali Yuga Poetics holds books as sacred receptacles of wisdom and guidance. Poetry's texts are illuminated—sometimes in gold, all kinds of colors that reappear in dream state. Kali Yuga practices the dreaming of ending wars, illness, famine, starvation, enmity, lawsuits, nuclear holocaust. Kali Yuga Poetics has contacts in high places who go against the grain. Kali Yuga Poetics cannot be bought. Kali Yuga Poetics brooks no disaster but meets disaster head on. Kali Yuga Poetics gets down with the winos back of Art Hardware store. Kali Yuga Poetics is put in her place by her Maya companeros, by the Apache brothers. Kali Yuga Poetics has seen her own death, She visualizes the charnel ground, the bony hag's skull. She sees flesh drop away, muscle drop away, sex drop away. Kali Yuga Poetics is never morbid. Kali Yuga Poetics writes all through the night. Kali Yuga Poetics manifests in 10 directions simultaneously. One, the domestic household front. Two, the school front where Kali Yuga students are trained to look at their own Kali Yuga minds. Three, the lovers' realm of intimate sweet discourse, passionate intercourse. Four, the desk, the edges of sanity, collage, compilation, language, loneliness. Five, the Information nets & highways & lines of exchange & debate, family talk, newspapers, The Poetry Project, Committee On Poetry, Burroughs Communications Systems, The Jack Kerouac School of Disembodied Poetics, the Committee to Bring

Work Back to Colorado. Six: with the children, ballgames, gamelan concerts, at the movies. Seven: the night again. Eight: Buddhist practice. Visualize this seed syllable that turns into a shining black crystal that enters your forehead, moves down your throat & lodges in the heart. Feel that stab in the heart at all times. Nine: You might need sleep. Kali Yuga Poetics has harnessed sleep into various dream yoga aspects that further your awareness. You can come & go as you like in this dream, speak to ancestors, others, enter at will, turn the flow another direction. Write it down. Ten: The Bardo. Follow the subtle lights not the bright bright lights of gaudy advertising.

Kali Yuga Poetics travels light. Kali Yuga Poetics visits caves. Kali Yuga Poetics goes into prisons. Kali Yuga Poetics does her best.

Poets if anyone does have to retain their dignity just like children even when they get yelled at or ignored.

    —Bernadette Mayer, *The White Squirrel Again*

Note From St. Francis

In the world today
there is
no world so attached as I am
to worlds.
All our hairyness
all our coarseness.
There is no texture in this
warmth I feel about
the creatures today.

We are gunning for extinction.
The sky is still bright
and all the animals running
for prehistoric sounds
believable in the passionate night.

    —Joseph Ceravolo

    Marked by death, who wants
to speak of the world conditions of this malady?
Its center a loneliness which pulls a human head
or an animal's body. We become something remotely com-
plicated, concentrating our presence against
this dimension. This is today how it is becoming. Woven
thousands of years ago in waiting. It is
integrated into loneliness, thriving upon the
self-forgetful like sleep. All days become a needle
in the way tracked. What is meant is evident.
The sun will outlast all the days we are vying for.
Trespassed upon into separation, our fate is
witnessed in its repetition.

    —Pam Rehm, from "Pericles, The Temptation to Exist"

Kali Yuga Poetics makes us nervous, driven, articulate witnesses on field of battle and poetry.

We do battle on Kali Yuga's speech-activity-continuity zone:

We are gunning for extinction

the sun will outlast all the days we are vying for

I mean none of this poet/warrior biz is actually comprehensible except that the metaphoricalness of reality is perceived.

> but my wounds which
> are the participants
> in what is not subject matter, but a poet's
> play, stage blood.

> They are the scourge of me—
> dear Iovis of the Fiery Night—Kali's slave
> into safer and shallower waters
> let me ride free.

— Anne Waldman, from *Iovis*

Was the presumption of public speech, he wondered, endlessly haunted by private misgiving? It was a question he could ill afford. Even as he teetered, only a hair's breadth away from the podium, teenage gangs were beginning to cluster at Block Station. He clamped a namesake lid on the recollection. The train slowed down to a halt. "I'm here," he said to himself, rapping the podium with his clenched right hand.

—Nathaniel Mackey, *The Creating of the Word*

Kali Yuga Poetics sets this down one season April/June in a dream.

Part III

Anne Waldman

Millennium Sutras

THE TWENTY-FOUR HOUR CHURCH OF ELVIS

I am interested in scoping out eccentric American locales with their vivid attendant particulars, "luminous details" as it were. Especially home-grown ones, those places & spots where myths combine to resound in outrageous play of contradiction, mixing levels of naivete, aberration, restlessness, fixation, icon worship and other manias that are particularly American. An amusing surrealism occurs that at the same time boggles the mind. The structures may be in place but what wild hybrids, what syncretic Towers of Babel may occur? How complex the web & network of phenomena both real and imagined. Often underscored by a basic hallucinatory religious fervor, alternately amusing & terrifying.

Some friends took me to the twenty-four hour Church of Elvis in Portland, Oregon. It was about 2 AM on a weeknight. We encountered first a cluttered, kitschy, storefront that spilled out into the street. It reminded me of Hindu shrines in India with offerings heaping up outside the temple gates. The area around the doorway was encrusted with an eclectic array of memorabilia, old parts of anything mechanical-imaginable-that-once-moved, broken plastic doll parts—distorted pink limbs, placid vacant eyes stare into eternity!—discarded toys, bits of rags and other cast-off garments, a plethora of textures & surfaces, miasmas of expendable stuff & garbage, a composite and compost of Americana detritus, touching amalgams of past, present & next expendable future.

The windows themselves continued this pastiche theme. It is said that the owner of the Church (which is also thought of as an "art gallery"), a woman, often inhabits

what surly uncivil men (woe-men) sprout forth
the sidewalks of San Francisco
to war
   future large as fright
   is all ~~your~~ own (ed)

official name: Republic of Iraq
capital: Baghdad
area: 169,235 sq mi
population: 16,476,000
language: Arabic
religion: Muslim, Christian
monetary unit: Iraqi dinar = 1,000 fils
land: in dispute in places but largely level region
   between Tigris & Euphrates
karma: Arabs settled 7th cent., Mongol invasion,
   British during WW I, Kurdish who were rightfully
   placed make demands, Baath party, wars with
   Iran, Gulf War

   ascent through the worlds
         ~~no solid I no solid I no solid ire no solid~~
~~right~~

page by desert bound
land?
land grab?

CENTO

Two gringos more or less between machos I was
crudo...

Left some in Lips?

The grenade blew her mink coat fifty yards...
gendarme stopped roughly
light blue suit stained down
Burroughs is dead
"interesting" reading
I was day like another quiet American
I was sabotage, ritual murder, uncouth beggar
I was unthinkable cold coffee cold American on the
floor
& smiles at you your shoes like obsidian mirrors
—that dreamy look—
& slow like stiff molasses says "Good to see you"
"Good night, sir" & me a sir?
I permitted to have locks
I, white-haired like the old Sugar Boss

Man he thought
was Yale Club
& set him on fire
that Old Reliable is late
Man dead on as winter night he thought
dead & the whole department is illegal
his black-out Lamb of God
talking right through flesh

thought....thought....
talking right through Total Oil the company
screen went dead
stained rather roughly
"Won't you have a beer?"
Regaining consciousness
all brothers of a cop said
"Hello, señor, you like my country yes?"
You didn't think I'd let you down, son. God?
pinch it himself most likely
Flying Saucers will be waiting
His line sweet & clear
But "I was not a man" saw right through this.

(in the voice from beyond of William S. Burroughs)

TORMIENTO DEL DESERTO

(this song to be accompanied with slow dirge-like drone)

> *"cold, cold smoked the bitch"*
> —American Pilot hitting an Iraqi Warplane

& you are brave
& you are sweeping
& precision carries you
like a dream

& your target is relevant
& your target is deceptive
& you think you can't get blinded
in a desert storm

& it's like the Bardo out here
you have no reference point
but equipment

You lived to do this
& the missiles are flaring
You've had your training
& you've been waiting

You perform with exactitude
But you could miss your target
You might fire at each other
You can't be sure of anything

You said goodbye
You walked away
You kissed the family
You went out the door

The Stealth was scary
But it stalked the enemy
& set a precedent
Launching a 2,000 lb. laser guided bomb

You don't think you're a killer
& you won't be a victim
This is the dilemma
You think you're a warrior

You thought you saw
Satan rising
He was alien, he practiced Islam
He was dark, he was evil

& where is compassion
in the form of a battalion
in the form of a Patriot
a mobile launcher, or how about Super
     Cobra or Tomahawk, first cruise missile?

Pyrotechnics,
surgical striking
Armageddon is hovering
Armadas are rising

Can you feel the desert
Does it turn your heart around
Will you dance like a Sufi
On the decimated ground

Perform like an angel
in the heat of the sun?
Perform like an angel
under the sun?

The crescent moon
You see it rising?
The moon of Rumi & all the prophets
on the horizon singing?

Will war ever be holy
Or is it just folly
Are we only reflections
of each other's pied beauty

O stop
The killing
It hurts the body
Destroys the psyche

The sand is blinding
Tiny particles bewitch your mind
The government binds you
It takes its toll from your hand

It takes your beauty
Takes innocence, takes youth
You could be back in the ghetto
Now fight for the truth

For the enemy bleeds
Out under the sun
Fragile eco-system recedes
Like a ghost

What is gained
For what was lost
What is gained
For what is lost?

Life is temporal
Try to be cautious
Be very careful on whom you tread
The option gets simple: you see your own death

It wreaks its havoc in an antithetical way
The desert is awesome
for its seeks its own blazing
Don't play with the devil, Saddam Hussein

& this is a story
It started so fast
one day in January
how many karmic aeons will it last

I wrote this song on an airplane
to meet my own perception
& transmute the suffering
of a desert storm.

January 1991
en route to
Bern, Switzerland

CITIPATI BLUES

Citipati are the dancing skeletons depicted in Tibetan Buddhist
and Tantric Hindu iconography, and are used as meditative visualizations to keep you on your toes. Memento mori ("remember
you must die") is the driving point here. One, if haunted by death,
might be more compassionate in life. This song was written as a
response to the terrifying arsenal deployed during Operation
Desert Storm.

U.S. Arsenal has over 20,000 nuclear weapons today
U.S. Arsenal has over 20,000 nuclear weapons today
It fires them up just to keep phantom enemy away

Enemy enemy where do you come from
Enemy enemy where do you come from
Are you just a hallucination
on the other side everyone's pointed (cocksure) gun

This gun is bigger than you could ever dream
O gun is deadlier than you could ever scheme
Its nuclear warhead trigger makes all the babies scream

Singing low down clinical depression
anti nuclear ballistic missile blues
Singing low down marrow sick hag-mother powered blues
Want radiation to end
We all put on our dancing shoes

We've been fast asleep naive doped up citizens all
We've been fast asleep or staring at the wall
While Pentagon mindset raves on
Got to get its money fill

Can't find the undaunted courage anywhere of a nuclear
    free virgin mind
Can't find the courage anywhere of a nuclear free virgin
    mind
Everybody's got so wordly
Want to blow it up leave this world behind

Planet's got aids O sing it to the skies
Planet's sick with aids O howl it to the skies
How to cure the patient before the patient dies

B-61, B-83, W-80-1 advanced cruise
W-80-0 Tomahawk, W-88 Trident II
Can't get my mind off these deadly missile blues

W-61 Interim Earth Penetrator Warhead
What business you got here
W-61 Interim Earth Penetrator Warhead
What business you got here
Gonna travel underground turn a bunker to a funeral pyre

Green Bee, Sky Horse are missiles of Taiwan
Condor II got South American on a run
Israel's three Jericho's make the walls come tumbling
    down

Wrathful mama sing those wrath from hell realm blues
Come up from your boneyard shake those rattling shoes
Citlpatl dancing on the grave of all those bombing crews

A-6 E Intruder, B-52 Stratofortress, Tomcat,
    Thunderbolt too
F-15 Eagle, F-111 Aardvark, F-4G Wild Weasel you're
    making me so blue
E-2C Hawkeye, AH-64 Apache, Chinook, Sea Cobra,
    Falcon what a stew

Alchemy alchemy O what ignorance wrought mankind
Transmuting gold to poison, it all begins with mind
Send plutonium back to the alembic purify the times

A woman gets high on her mountaintop
sings anti-missile put down blues
She can't keep her tongue from nagging, sing low down
    anti-nuclear hag wrought blues
But too late for that reversal
Just keep dancing as the cancer brews

Mama mama wrathful mama blues
Come up from the boneyard shake those rattling shoes
Citipati dancing on the graves of all us ignorant fools!

PART PRIMA DONNA

Mortify the villain
but a kind of dolor mother felt antiquated, no I mean
"anticipated"

        Propose to her—his?—O Doctor!—
Equivalent?

if this principal part is wasted on X, then...

    if you come to me, give me all!!!!!!!!!!!!!!!!!

if, if if, if, if

this "if" quest stresses factors, move & oblivion

I like all this "if" stuff but frankly Beatrice is all
the book I need

in hermetic sense

in direst day, Bosnia

in doctrinaire reality quotient

& you are fluctuating, I mean "articulated"

O dear, o dear, o dear

or schooled in all the mother I need

A rest, a rest I need

PROLOGOMENON TO A CONTIGUOUS PARTICLE
some definitions

an aside, a blunt instrument

informer:
side by side with broom

traps only some avoid
about paranoia & an object

this lesson: magnets

secular mimeticism
means
to answer slowly

cloth for the kitchen?
not cozy

bits of tea
equals
a burning tribal meditation

tiny filaments of dream:
the one with a revolver in it
sleeve of care
wrapping foil
closeted before dawn
baskets

a trifle longer?
saw, a fixing saw

mend:
I saw the snake slip away

sweep:
I saw the cracks between

hewn & covered
like a wagon

or tiled
candle

tree doctor stands erect
warm soiled hands

glass observed
a blackening stem

matter of fact
stove art

window repression:
dust bin

another human
used to swim here

illudere: to mock

poetry:
cloudy
or
exquisitely made

TRANSFORMER

*When we fall in love we're going toward revelation
we're falling into the Universe
in Universe Mnemosyne
Transform the story
of my past-all-surrounds-me.*

The Queen of the Trick Roller, Miami Nelson, said this morning: "You might not be the Queen of the Trick Roller, but you're certainly the most experienced Parking Lot Commando I can recall!" The Queen of the Parking Lot was partially insulted and bopped her one playfully, with a rolled-up newspaper: "Oh Dottie, you're a card!"

reads Sports

flesh check blanket distributes nicely under bearlike friend
splayed out in sun

summer's chirping bird pauses...

the stream moves, moving, moves the garden spinach all along

shadows of prehistoric ferns will mention Wall Street, Salina Star Route, Colorado, shadows of plants on your body

I back up

Back in New York another companion absorbs my adolescence

Happy to be here in a bundle, not dying of radiation

Summer couples line the road in sexual torpor,
read "sexual," I lecture on new-found celibacy,
how it accounts for taking on all sentience in the
world...

Hot stuff at Rocky Flats

A man kisses my hand and intrudes

"This is the bedroom," she bristles.

He held me. She cornered me. He interrupted us.
She moved away. He loved me. He held me. He
left me. He interviewed me. She bristled. I moved
downstairs.

For the beginning: He married me. He cornered
me. He moved away. I was always playing prince
and the heart's not even a little bird is reminding
me...

Never cease to astonish a whole family goes out
the window of a $90-a-day motel in Salt Lake City
unable to cope after father, a god incarnate, takes
himself out of this world

                                       while
handicapped people trapped in a bus in Quebec
scream and tourists look on chuckling, snapping
pictures.

You might say the severe denial of the body
through history is this machine recording and no
place to put the mind like footprints of that bird in
the sky. True?

BURNT OUT YEARS AGO CATHEDRAL

this is my object

smell of new moon hay

this is it: elevator with two kids I'm here I'm here

this is my object: a golden dome in Iowa

this is my object

a prison

a railroad apartment

this is my dream I'm in it

they cut open my mother

they cut open my father

they cut open my brother

a sleep shade on

my head exploded

this is my object: a crystal ball

all around the edges of a tent

wind flapping the canvas white room

this is my object a golden torah

this is my dream:

coming back at night the tiny black flashlight

it is a good guy, a good doll

hugging as pelvis please preacher, please police

the West Suede highway

wake up or think I wake

Bob in a park this is his dream

a heart attack across generations

extra soft

burnt out years ago Cathedral

all alone eyes watching me

this is my sacred object

this is my dream

when I was in the army

cheapo eveready

my object is my shawl

I'm here & I'm here

These pieces of string aren't holding anything
together

But they are part of the design

AWAKE [UP]

jungle rising into sky

tropical bugs & night buzz

I lost my water

I lost my way there

There were stones in front of my eyes

No flashlight but a love box, full of the coins of love

the 3 D of the computer keys

resilient magics

or mortifications

SHAKE UP

someone died

& then a cat dies

***

clan life was reincarnation

clan life held us her, located, a place to be

place?

& if you believe this sort of thing

you could enter inside cat

place

placed

placate

a place to be

it was wide like a river can be and currenting

currenty, the child said

wide like this river

clan life was being a beaver in the mushroom
gulch place

clan life was independent of the rest of it

I sweep my hand away to show you the rest

clan life was exciting it was the only life

because we were together, we were clan

not brother not sister all of that too but clan
clan like a token range clay made
clan like normal propensity
what could last some might say
or not, the inbred-ness of it
clan blind
bristle of clan in morning everyone hungry
or wanting to agree but not

I would I could

leader? that was the buddiness of elder

elder was a history

was an old story

carried the blame

responsibility?

woke to duty because it was a clan

needed governance?

clan not so obscure when you think on it

tribes are different

how?

tribes are summation

& have the animals intact

& wild toon nut named & imitated

clan might come later

beaver clan, bring back the industry of beaver

ANNA

*This makes the difference between single
lines and broad stomachs*
—Gertrude Stein

If it had not been a light white

It was a crest upslanting
The sudden wound is the spoon

Found herself in peace of the dot
Wide chalk, all of this combing
Taken the place
And nervous bed rows

Anna did not
Anna did not
Anna did vote

Anna did the friend
This is not tardy

All sorts of mounted reserves
And loud presidential volumes
And nervous bed rows

This friend was dark
Very easy in a shelter
With little ins and red
A virgin a whole virgin

Very good to friend the careless
Between old ladies and mild colds

Hardly answer anything
It shuts & it lifts
And nervous bed rows

Anna spread into nothing
Anna spread into nothing
All go fairly well

Then be reckless be reckless
This is no dark custom

PARITY

what's at stake
　　the future & its readings

infinite room
　　a stupid woman

hard & unrelenting
　　her selfish suffering

remarkable narcissism
　　hotter than law

injustice?
　　its own reward

human delusion
　　an angry face

prison strum
　　idiot compassion

BONEYARD

How many fancy packages with designer goods,
built-in obsolescence, objects do I have to buy and wrap
>how many bows to show you how much I care
>>(put it all out in the yard, out in the boneyard, the giant
>>heap)
How many things, shiny and clean, certified,
homogenized, sentimentalized have to be manifested
>here?
>>(put them out on the charnel ground, the boneyard, the
>>primordial heap)
How many useless material goods, unrecyclable goods
you already have a dozen of them, you already have a life-
>time of...
—have to find a shelf a drawer a cabinet to wear out their
>lonely span
(out in the yard, out in the boneyard, a giant heap)

Coming empty-handed now
Nothing in hand

Things pollute the land
Clog the highways
Fill the nooks and crannies of our world

Dead meat now
Tinsel, conjurers tricks, illusions
Out in the boneyard, the charnel ground
pile them up
out in the yard
out in the boneyard

NO CHILD'S UTOPIA

Election off the blade of life of Palestine
lectare: what is this doing to our reading populus?
settle the scores
ions, negative, a semblance of...? wilt & power
a colder war a colder colder war

Go along with it never makes the ritual abort but it wakes to make you do it then it does you in the blink of dynasty's eye, old power old pull old atavistic eye wanders down a lonely road and roads away to crypt's established ground. Political rant or rave. Out in a city now, the urban density will take out more than a few lives. You could make a gory bath, a blood bath, a *ganachakra* (feast) of grisly gore. You want to scream it: grisly grisly grisly grisly gore. Smell it? Grisly gore. Charged & camouflaged to the enemy's rank, Israeli coat of arms and then you blow yourself up in remembrance of a meal, a bread, a lover you never could have time for running the blast, a taste, as slight accorded the back to cellular land. You? You? I did not know a one of them. I'll never know a one of them. I'll never land there but back in time Beirut 1972, a six day war. You'd better not cry out, or single yourself out now you are standing in an interstice of scenario you've no right of understanding and yet do that to rise up. Land a mine. Land could never be grabbed who had it might have mighted it and the wake of a thousand sucked off dreams. What is a Mother Country? bordered, a place you set yr satyr feet to cultivate, the simple shade is drawn. Hide in here, hide in the cloak. How will this make a country work? It must be two countries, equal & free.

Then learn yourself good—a rhetoric approval won't gainsay then drop in a bucket the Hamas agenda. Stirred up to the pearly gates of an impossible heaven & you are young, bestial because you saw too much hunger, oppression, exhaustion (the I Ching hexagram affords a classic rap). No shield for the terrorist, confiscate his house or beat his family down, what could make you do it become human bomb become a walking bomb for Allah's heaven? That blue iznic tiled recompense naught but blood and bits of flesh blast or scattered on the micro-dot screen no won't reduce to that phobia's grace but let it sound bleaker not to be done aplomb the man can't help it because of what so many suffered then conditioned you've got to see it all ways won't preach a bottom line who's all glitched innocents, the little ones dressed for Purim won't get off on this photo that cast because the casted down are forever accosted 2 more dead in the lexicon. Then martyred on International TV. Pass by, the book. Meant to merely record the symptoms of a time gone mad in reaction because the tyrants swept in and where were you to go disenfranchise the whole wild real scene, not a stage set, not a dream. This book does not agree with my book. This religion does not agree with that one. Then there's always a hidden agenda.

I'm my Arab hip I am my blown out Ethiopian brains I am nuked Israeli I am the fragments of no more no man's no woman's no child's utopia and still not writing of cry revenge. But would or could.

dictate: the blade-life
walk a fine line
you live off headlines
go made with rage
capitalist excruciating "karma" gets you
the cold
eye
lens you wish to focus
focus, focus again on something beautiful
breathe now, breathe steadily now
lost on all fronts
or slow this scenario down
work or does it
rave for the right to get inside
my own unpacified brain
the newspaper is a blade is a book is a blade.

NEGRONI O'HARA

Drinking alcohol is not a fashionable nor as carefree as it used to "seem." This is for those with a taste for the cocktail hour. (It helps to be in love.)

There's the wonderful Frank O'Hara poem, "Having a Coke with You" in which O'Hara extols the pleasure of a certain someone's company while imbibing America's favorite cola together, declaring it being "even more fun than going to San Sebastian, Irun, Hendaye, Biarritz, Bayonne/or even being sick to my stomach on the Travesara de Gracia in Barcelona," and also the poem "Beer for Breakfast" where he writes "I give a cocktail in the bathroom, everyone gets wet/it's very beachy." These are just a few examples, there being endless references to drinks of all kinds throughout the O'Hara canon. "He gets up, lights a cigarette, puts fire/under the coffee" ("Those Who Are Dreaming, A Play About St. Paul"). In "To The Music of Paul Bowles": "...and Maxine said WAIT/which meant another vodka and campari." But being told in the sixties (by Ted Berrigan) that "Negronis are Frank's favorite drink!" and actually seeing, I think, him drink one or some similar concoction at a Bill Berkson party many moons ago, and knowing Campari & vodka are getting close to what constitutes a true Negroni, and seeing how much mention of Vermouth O'Hara's got all over the place, I decided to search out this triple-whammy-elixir in various lounges, bars, restaurants of the world. The drink hails from Italy and means "dark" or "black" and seems to still find some takers (I drank Grappa over there, it's cheaper, although Grappa is Not a cocktail). But it's an obscure request in most places. This has been a many decades project & most bartenders think I'm giving them some kind of *test.* This is a drink for people who still enjoy martinis (& Frank O'Hara's poetry). My version:

Campari—1 jigger
Vodka—1 jigger
A generous dash of Vermouth (chilled)
Pour over 3 cubes of ice
Add a slice of fresh lime peel & splash of Bitters

ENTREATY

You will find a lot of independence and fierce individualism among the population, but it doesn't show up much in the dominant culture, that is, the culture that actually makes decisions and controls.

***

The political arena is not enough, but even the engagement of the population in the political area would be useful progress toward democracy in the United Sates. By that I mean not just watching the candidates on television and clapping for them, but actual participation, real participation in formation of programs, in meaningful selection and recall of representatives, etc.

—Noam Chomsky

prayer to
flick of eyelash
glance
bow
leer
look in one's paranoid eyes
we gathered inside the room
clay (for art)
mile (for belly)
public school as birthrite
citizenry
elbow in ribs
poke
kick
touch

(we pull off Mrs. Mulherne's wig)
a *communitas* of
flare
rockets
signals
tone of a voice
the day we got letters back from Albert Einstein (3rd
grade)
a modest man
a moment of silent pantomime
& for the dead in war
& of hunger
flag-particles
I marched
read a poem on Arbor Day
I marched
& pledged allegiance to other people

       that some do not control (bespeak) the mood is
       a metaphorical mantra:

OM PARTICIPATE AH

HUM!

CLOSE TO HOME
Revelation Song for Steven Taylor

(He said)
Be careful who you tell what you tell
Your secrets will not make you free
But life is short, the sun goes out
Why dwell in para noi a-ee?

The clos'd safe, the clos'd vault
The clos'd gun where panic dwells
The light inside a terrorist's eye
Where does it lead, to suicides' hell?

Poetry holds some funny truths
And lover's kiss doth trigger bliss
The work you do unties the knot
& text you write not run amiss

Askew, amiss dense commodified world
Material sweat, material strife
Poisonous things won't make you free
Better you live a simple life

I see what I say on my poet's page
I sing it to you on the darkening hour
And planet's colors all come to light
With discriminating eye of the gatherer, the hunter.

DHARMA LECTURE

"Delusion will do the work for you if you don't wake up"

Tibetan lama's wincing details describe coolie life
Calcutta's Howrah station
one sooty shirt, weather hot or cold
asleep on platform
whistle blows

hop to hop to! conditioned ghost

Coolie piles but fraction of your possessions on poor
head for a few tossed rupees
"Be content with what you have"

Slice of grey Tilburg sky out shrine room window
crossed with wires & chimneys

Bespectacled Dalai Lama dignifies wall

Lama Gelek holds up Chandrakirti's glass of water
"It's undrinkable poison to the insatiable hungry ghost,
amrita to the gods,
just okay—(but is it? laced with plutonium?)
—for us humans"

You are what you perceive.

A LETTER to intent magazine

To go a bit further: The description and experience of "cold hell" in Tibetan Buddhist psychology is of interest in contrast to the "otherwise abstract Tibetan 'cold hell' Charles Olson found in Waddell" (*intent,* Jack Clarke, Winter/Spring 1991), and we find in Tom Clark's Olson biography as well. These notes are just for the record, since I merely want to point out the *precision* of Padmasambhava's "text." The "cold hell" is an icy world in which everything is completely frozen. From the psychological point of view, one's energy has shut down, and refuses to communicate at all. The environment frosts over. In the *Bardo Thotrol*, The Tibetan Book of The Dead, we encounter this bleak proscription:

If you are going to be reborn as a hell being you will hear songs sung by those of evil karma, or you will have to enter helplessly, or you will feel that you have gone into a dark land, with black and red houses, black pits and roads. If you go there you will enter hell and experience unbearable suffering through heat and cold from which you will never get out.

One is there instructed, before possible rebirth, to *"close the womb entance and think of resistance."*

No wonder.

The Book of The Dead speaks of the "soft-smoking" light of hell beings. When one's consciousness—after death and free of body—is wandering, it tends to be attracted to a soft, gentle light, rather than an intense blinding one. The cowardly attraction to the "safe" light refers to the inviting

111

path of neurotic veils, accumulated by acts of both mental and violent physical agression.

Traditionally there are 8 hot hells, 8 cold hells, and 2 neighboring hells. The 8 cold hells are Arbuda, Nirarbuda, Atata, Hahava, Huhura, Utpala, Padma, and Mahapadma. The first 2 hells get their names from the hideous changes that appear on the bodies of the inhabitants. Because of unbearable coldness, blisters rise on their bodies and burst. The next 3 hells are named from cries of being pained by the untenable cold there. Of the last 3, one has the color of green bark & is split into 5 or 6 openings like a blue lotus (*utpala*); another is shaded from blue to red and has 10 or more openings, like a red lotus (*padma*) & the third is a deep red color and is split into more than one hundred openings like a great lotus (*mahapadma*). These 3 hells derive their names from changes appearing on the bodies as well. Terrifying putrefactions of all kinds!

The span of life in these cold hells is also quite exact:

> *When every hundred years out of a sesame store*
> *One sesame grain is taken and this store is emptied*
> *The time elapsed is the span of life in Arbuda hell*
> *That in other hells is twenty times greater*

From some point of view, the poet might recognize his/her mental condition in the Tibetan Buddhist imagination.

Warmly,
AW

Source: *Gampopa's Jewel Ornament of Liberation*

HEAT IS ON

As we sit gazing into the next millennium not so far away—as poets, scholars, meditators, artists, musicians—the Radical Christian Right (which includes the vast grassroots organization the Christian Coaltion—the powerful brainchild of televangelist Pat Robertson—as well as Colorado for Family Values based in Colorado Springs) is hard at work across the country promoting its agenda of virulent intolerance. No matter the recent outcome of Amendment 2—now most certainly a positive outcome and a temporary victory for gay & lesbians' rights—these newly sprouting organizations will skillfully and ruthlessly pursue their ultimate goal of amassing considerable political power. The struggle isn't over, dear consociates. We need to raise our "antennae-of-the-race"-consciousness and check this busy scene out. The high tech born-again computers are clicking away, the signatures and dollars are rolling in. There is a plan afoot in every state of this country to move forward on many fronts—including anti-abortion, harassment of health care providers, to oppose repeal of the military's ban on homosexuality, to censor curricula from the public schools, to mandate the teaching of the Biblical account of Creation in public school biology classrooms, to rescind gay and lesbian rights in nine states, censor popular entertainment and literature, to just say no to adolescent sex initiatives, to ban discussion of AIDS from public school, to gear political moves to capture key positions on school boards etc etc. Alarming progress has been made on these many fronts. The Radical Christain Right, festering under the presidencies of Reagan and Bush, was never happy with the policy changes that resulted after swinging the election to the Republicans and felt that the social agenda they proposed so adamantly was never properly enacted. The abortion issue, their pet obsession was not taken seriously enough. They retrenched and came up with a clearer offensive. Now they are on the move with a vengeance. It's a crusade, a holy war with very clever strategies—work from the grassroots up. What do poets do when the devil's so obviously at the door. Howl? Get the facts? Write letters? Talk & complain about the dread Kali Yuga? I write from the Outrider School, the Disembodied Poetics school of Zen Zone Poetics. Be creative in your efforts. Get the facts straight. Write out of your gentle Boddhisattvaic Negative Capability to transform these evil vibes coming at you from all sides. Champion the underclass, the underdog, minority rights. O holier war! The gay rallies planned all over the nation give us heart. The first gay couple pulled up in a limo at the Boulder High School prom this year and no one booed!

Summer Writing Program
The Jack Kerouac School of Disembodied Poetics
1993

KALACHAKRA DREAM

"Do you know the five nectars?"

"Yes," I reply to T., "Semen, marrow, blood, urine, feces."

"And the dieties in unison?"

"Kalachakra & Vishvamata. Is this a Buddhist quiz?"

We are viewing these powerful deities together, looking upward at their visualized bodies, like holograms. A HUM, turning into a five-pronged vajra joins blue-skinned Kalachkra's secret place, and a *phat!* covers his penis-hole. An AH rests at yellow-skinned Vishvamata's secret place, transforming into a red lotus, and a *phat!* her vagina.

Could this be us copulating, witholding ourselves in some gone trantric imagined realm? (Of course these visualizations are quite traditional.) But he was always more like a brother.

I've been worried about T., not having seen him in so long. Has he been a homeless vagabond? He looks it, face sooty & weathered, clothes soiled. He wears a dirty rainbow-hued poncho of coarse wool. Yet warm. And studying it, I say "the toughest fiber," thinking of his sharp mind. His voice is aged, yet instilling the usual irony—his quirky thought. He proffers a flask. "Fibber?" "Tiber?" Now there are crowds of devotees coming between us. We will not get drunk together.

"What are the four night appearances because if you know I'm imitating one of those, ha!"

I recite to myself: *smoke, sparks, flame of a butter lamp,* hurrying my thinking over the din of exuberant yogins (men & women, hair matted, eyes wide).

"Butter lamp!" I cry, and he's gone.

....

Old student

> *to fathom lost night*

or chart tide & time, eclipses of the moon

> *grinding dharma-wheels where gods are swift*

interstices of poverty & desire

let's mount the illusory dream....a lamp, a candle

> *How fare thee—well?*

REVOLUTION AS A TERM THAT
TURNS SO MANY WAYS

I am an exile
transforming
energy
Bow to history
personality,
the industrial revolution,
French too, bow to William Wordsworth's French Honey,
Bow to the proper use of energy,
Does one war for love, die of it?
See the
turn
in
the molecules,
ah where does it lead & do we like it?
no don't don't like it no it fashions heartbreak,
destroys…

NO BLOOD FOR OIL

"The most sublime act is to set another before you"

"For Man has closed himself up, till he sees all things
thro' narrow chinks of his cavern"

BORN AGAIN BLUES

Orphaned orphaned Mommy & Daddy done gone
(repeat)
I've got that inner traumatized American white child
within wanna wail all night long

She's got a wrinkled hag's body itching & bitching
inside
(repeat)
She's gonna come out raging & demonize the country-
side

Born again born again let those fundamentalist inner
child demons pollute the sky
(repeat)
I'm gonna burn all you pro-choice queer atheists just
to see you fry

Life's no fun unless you're fighting the lord god's holy
war
(repeat)
He's got a mean eye-for-an-eye doctrine—it says
you burn in the Bible—
save you from from Satan's door

Amendment 2s Measure 9s all around the USA
(again)
See the laws change, get on the school boards give
creationists, bigots, racists, the right o' way

O I'm born again born again you got see it my
     escatological way
(repeat)
I've got a right to sing the blues too get everyone on
     their knees 'n pray

But in the dark of night I just can't find any peace
Out on the street by day I'm haunted by this born
     again theistic fundamentalist disease
So consumed hating phantom enemy can't find any
     release

Born again born again shriek it to the skies
(repeat)
Got that born again inner demon child inside telling
     me crazy lies.

VERSION FROM THE MAN YOSHU
OR
COLLECTION OF 10,000 LEAVES

*(oldest Japanese Anthology of poetry
compiled mid 8th Century)*

At night when rain beats down
driven by wind
At night when snowflakes & sleety rain beat
down
I feel helpless, cold
I nibble at a rock of salt
Sip hot exhausted dregs of saké
Cough, stroke my scant beard
And say with pride
Heh there's no one as good as me!
But I'm shivering
I pull up my stringy bedclothes
The night is cold & bitter
I think: there are those poorer
whose parents must be cold & hungry too
Women & children begging and crying
How do you get through life?
They say heaven & earth are vast
This world looks narrow to me
The sun & moon are supposed to be bright
They never shine for me
Is everybody in the same boat? just me?
I had a precious human birth
no meaner than the next one
But now I'm in tatters

These rags are like weeds waving in the sea &
hang loosely from my scrawny body
I lie on staw spread on bare earth
under a sunken roof
Walls collapse
My parents are at my pillow
Family at my feet
Huddled in deperate grief & tears
We've got no fire
Not a grain to cook
A spider spins her web in the pot
We moan like the night thrush
The village boss comes to our sleeping place
& prods us with a stick, growls for dues
Is it always so hopeless,
the way of this world?

OBIT

necrology?   death roll?
casualty list?
body count?
what's allowed
in a corpse of a century,
to fathom
to dream on
                what got plundered

but we live, *loved*
"party" is not a word I'd think to summon
what is the summation of
the nightmare
or
dream
who puts it thus away
when we're   to fathom
a speculation
what's gone
undone
for a tangle
(tango)
this Hundred Year Meditation ....

it was a moment
it was a golden eye-blink
it was a microdot—one galaxy's inbreath
one sigh
one gesture of seduction

one rapt pause
several comets
eclipse, eclipse, eclipse
it was the shrug of Brahma's shoulder
creak of Isis' oar
heave of a chest
lonely cough
her sidelong glance
her fancy gait
will she kiss her lover?
her gasp—it is bad? is the news bad?
they make love at dawn
"time" explodes
his quizzical look
what news, Claudius?
the end of a movie
someone dies
it was a dart of passion
it was a conjunct of earth & sky
the earth stood still
a scream
then falters
it was over & it was beginning
it was over it was war it was war it was war
it is war
it was war
no
it is war
it is the set-up for war
the frame up ⎯

it was a long time
Neptune rules

*

the century grows on us
poets invent language
perceptions collide
I hear the mitocondria shift in my dna
part of it was part of my history
& part of it was elsewhere
& Gertrude Stein said
America was the oldest country
because it entered the 20th century first
I saw the century unfold & die
I saw it unfold from within America
it was part of me
it made me what I am
I am war I was war I am war
 American made
I am power & eyes & parables
I will close my fist & raise it to the first cause
I will fight
I will not survive
No
I am survivor
but I forgot what I just said to you
I forgot something
no
I forgot
I forgot something

amnesia of holocaust
amnesia for war & war & more war
witness the end of Nature
I want to forget her beauties
because I helped destroy them
nothing will ever be the same
there is no topsoil left in the world
& many species extinct....

*

from the vantage point of
power & power & more power
see with ancient eyes
because it would be the first to die
we'll die in America first
are we modern,
are we modern yet?
someone tell us
are we the post-modern Dark Ages yet?
it is simply dialectical materialism
it is the charnel ground
many jackals roam about
& feast on the bloody severed limbs of
1. desire
2. hope & fear
real live bodies
it was divide & conquer
it was glory glory & more glory
what genomes?
what clones?

what could we ever do to outdo our century

*

made love this century
gave birth this century
walked this century
laughed this century
protested Rocky Flats this century
dreamed the rapids came this century
dreamed a lamp to light the way—
O Nirvana of the little lamp!
meditated this century—hey ho the happy yogini!
raged on stage this century
founded a school this century
stomped on the corpse of ego this century
became an ego-maniac this century
watched good folks die this century
buried a mother, buried a father, buried a best friend

set flames to the corpses on the charnel ground
are they really planning to create life from the
ovaries of unborn fetuses this century?

took a powder this century
took a powder down the information highway.

INSURRECTION: LOS ANGELES

Torrent to torment to meet the fire there. To burn, burn. To meet the man. Meet the down-the-street-man behind-it-all-man. Point of economic reference? Damn their toys! Not referee or reference spike. Rake the coals over. Burn, burn. It was a pointed telling it was a hurt to all it was hurting all. I was wild and fire was all around. "I could not breathe." "I saw it coming." "Arm the brothers." Nostril was flaring. Flatten out the time, the fire all around. Damn their Orient. On sight a light who knows how long it smokes. It smolders in a brute way. A king is much maligned. Thy rod & staff no longer comfort still. Rod & burn. A king is beaten, spike & rod to come down on a back, on a head. No one to head off. No wise leaders. Supreme white whitens a cause. Kill the king. What picture got knighted here? Who is speaking? Sweep the glass. Sound of a heart shattered. "All my hopes & dreams. My little life (I put it all in the store) go up in smoke."

Blame the mounted. Blame the sound a system makes. Blame o cast a blame an eye to pain. Go back in centuries old keep down their might and fury leash now you pay pay up you pay you pay.

Child bends over to retrieve her rubble toy. Pictures blur. Objects which are symbols a hell makes real. Now you pay up you pay you pay.

CANTICHE

Respective spheres,
the danger is past
a lot of time spent driving
Independence of women means
that on my fingers you can't tell
where she's been—Morocco?
stained with henna...
"You are speaking to me?"
absence of wind
Why are we driving there:
Lago di Como
You said we "must"
you said *"Death is naked*
not masked by laughter or charm"
Speaking in English now
turn pale, drive faster,
more ground to cover
find the "right place"
all night from Vienna, then
all night from Munich
glare at the continual miracle
of unconventional behaviour
Ours? in any mind

I want to write about
a way of seeing you & everyone else
Sleek packaging, hot new items,
imperious waiters, Euro-dollars
passersby who sing & offer vittles
Meanwhile the earth turns
in its death-dance lining up little
or no options to survive
out in a beautful desert
"Are you sure?" "Are you strange?"
You want me here meeting relatives
& for the exotic drive
through medieval towns
We stop, take turns sleeping
observe details
Man at petrol station
looks at me, wonders
nationality, *she married?*
Places cry out for
romance, celebration & recognition
because we are travelling inside them
salvation from an imposition of
weaponry & its scents
Invisible, deathly amrita

permeates the air
as axis powers shift their deadly intentions
Why doesn't it all go up in smoke?
Wonder who vacationed here in earnest
What emperors hovered through exacting tributes
with every symptom of success
once native to an exotic air
"I think you are très difficile"
(exasperating smile)
Standing impatiently as if wishing to leave
resulting in another way around
Il Duomo is sanctuary
because estranged from native tongues
ourselves & any other comparison
we are proud, religious
"You are welcome to all the handles in my world!"
What does that mean?
You notice my suntanned arms,
dark glasses, moist eyes, American gaze
proffer a drink inside villages small & empty
How does it happen settling down to
relax in fascination of your promise
to be comrades?
It begins with fear of leaving home

& a gentleman complained
how the olive oil wasn't
"up to snuff" in his salad travelling alone
wishing the waiter were a wife
Our valise is light & lonely
We are dwarfed by mountain & lake
They speak to us, chasten us
"You are too new, too modern
You get tipsy on the wine we provide
You forget how to struggle
To remain artists get headaches
& don't put in an appearance
Stick with nocturnal research get good at it!"
Why do these steeples point skyward?
What religious architect dwells there?
We are in an *opera buffa*
carried away by our own projected voices
which again speak of light:
It is writing and speaking of light
that carries us, eyes closed
in a kind of trance now
Nearer to the lake
further off from ourselves.

Part IV

Jack Collom

This Morning's Revolution

RECIPE FOR A MOUSE

Take atoms of carbon, hydrogen, oxygen,
silicon, phosphorus, etc. etc., combine into
amino acids, let simmer
for a billion years
till strings of proteins &
dioxyribonucleic acid form
double helixes of subconscious
intelligence—hot as the sun
cool as the moon
let simmer, let grow, pour into a ball,
into a wet blue splash, let it go,
let it grow
3 billion years
thru protozoan particles floating in a primal soup
of light & death
& sex & desire & magic &
beautiful by-products
thru canopies & rainbows gratuitous
heave onto land
sand, ferns, sharp rocks
under dinosaurian rumbles, under, thru
into shadow
suddenly
2 little eyes
under a leaf—
add 1/2 cup blood
slice bulk hair to delicate threads of fur, dispose

round
twist tiny pink muscles
insert
white bones like calcium toothpicks
cook up tiny organs
heart, liver, lungs
& brain—fold mystery leaves
& synapse jumps,
cells—ea. a soft natural factory
of wild civility
fold them, stroke
electricity into the trembling small handful
breathe
into it—find more magic
than you have.
let it go.

tell stories
Mickey Mouse, elephants, rascals, jokesters,
cheesewits, let it all flow over
the genuine mouse
whose every move
is echoed in the stars
& spaces between.

serve.

Death of Mouse, & Mice, & More

The death of mice is common, lovely, below perception.
The mouse died.
Half-eaten by a cat, nuthouse known as domestication,
    wherein the kill is stretched in a long dotted line
    between whim & necessity.
The mouse died.
Breathing civilized dust, particulates, sulfur dioxide,
    lead, nitrogen oxides, volatile organics, ozone from
    photochemical smog, the heart failing and falling
    through blackness, slow ache replacing lungs.
Sliced by machine raggedly in square field.
Died.
Sucking in carbon monoxide at a crossroads. Silver pipes.
Drowned by rash of coastal tides in upward rush of
    heat, loss of the local to big spread effect.
Clog of piled nitrates. Sheer arsenic.
Never-born, as life-rich soil washed away & no green
    occurred. Grisly absence.
Died contemplating dead lake after dead lake, went
    blind in triplicate.
Strangled by plastic wrappers.
Died due to polychlorinated biphenyl toxicity in body
    fat ruining exploratory thought.
Petrochemical-based tumors brutalizing light cells.
Died from eating radioactive fescue seeds—flesh woven,
    twined, laced, knitted, spliced, plaited, warped,
    sprained, wrenched, disjointed, contorted, screwed,
    perverted, garbled, mutilated, fudged, rent, falsified.

Died, stomach curdled to white circles by stupid dust.
Whisked out space-hole behind chlorofluorocarbons
    button-pushed.
Died flattened at all costs by abstractions of concrete.
Died with eyes, ears, tongue ladled burning caustic for
    a possible cosmetic liquid.
Ultraviolet fry. Bubbled skin.
Died of no-harmony choking spirit, since no fact is lost
    in smallness.
Died of chewing wads of money, poison green ink suf-
    fusing perfect muscles.
Died of delicacy lost.
The mouse died, pumped full of phosphates.
Died dwindling down into hard geometry.
Died of spottiness crushing pink exactitude.
Died in oily tricks that made the moment spread like butter.
Died of mercury racing coldly through red rounds of
    white blood.
Died of possibilities ricocheting way past pale finger-
    tips & red claws.
Died in artificial dots, in cacophonies of pain, a wonder
    of warning, a counterpoint, perimeter of grace get-
    ting twisted to condition, thus to whole shape, in
    which the mouse died.
& did it ever live? Bright eyes, touch & thought? Yes.

sestina (6-1-87)

money
this
you
go
and
hot

hot
money
and
this
go
you

you
hot
go
money
this
and

and
you
this
hot
money
go

go
and
money
you
hot
this

this
go
hot
and
you
money

money this
you go
and hot

this morning's revolution

Revolution!
turn it around
to *revolución*, translation
turn it around
to No it ulo ver, polarization
un shun ocean lotion ovation volition evolution
Revolution!
I gotta notion—revolution!
revolution of a notion—
I notion up a motion that a portion of the ocean, whose
location is a caution (the omission of flotation), Land o'
Goshen, BE a potion, osculation & devotion, to any
Trojan beach!
so what accumulation is the base initiation of Revolt?
ovulation variation, permutation?
expedition from perdition?
frustration & elation of a nation?
peregrination of exception to emendation?
hallucination of progression?
illusion libation of alienation?
lack of station in creation?
option revelation in the microspheric convolution?
Incompletion?
the fact that something's fucked-up like death in a
    pool & gotta be dealt with?
everything's a revolution
universe a revolution

molecule a revolution
starry night a revolution
hemisphere a revolution
every day a revolution
getting up a revolution
brushing teeth massaging hair & rolling eye
toilet waters revolution
semiotics revolution
the semantic revolution
galileo revolution
endless dervish revolution &
the great Big Bang is whirling in its grave
hypnotism revolution
hologramic revolution
& Revolution's every revolution's never repetition, rhythm
rolls, & comes up different, it's a spiral, that's the way it
goes, mirror image, something's sitting there trying to
freeze its own parabola, squashing the particles of
groundlife, maybe people, taking people to portend,
portray, all popping chemicals, sporting indubitable
perimeter, par'mecium amoeba roundworm poplar
petunia quetzal & parrot any-colored panther pouncing
bouncing peering popeyed in the shadow—so this sitting something gotta go, gotta flip, it'll *be* there, it'll be
buried in the circle, in the circle's secret circle, shak-
ing in the substance, but it's gotta go, netherworld
somersault, *it'll* be back, a little different, gotta
turn/or/burn something new rising from the bottom.

To the tune of "Amazing Grace"

Appointed soil / sole ground of life
Slow growth since coastal dawn
      So recently your stuff was rife
      And soon O nearly gone

———

Eight hundred kinds / of birds delight
The North American air
      But forests're felled in a money-fight
      There'll be no nesting there

———

The western bluebird / sang among
The February sage
      Its warbles sweet were roundly flung
      Howe'er the snow did rage

———

A little liquid / trickles down
The thinness of the Platte
       A million burghers swell the town
       And that's the end of that

——

The fox squirrel's tail / jerks light as air
Shows feathery orange core
       The brown face dressed in short, flat hair
       Provides the either/or

——

"Hey, Mother Nature / Father Time
Is running up the road!"
       "He'll never come," she said in rhyme
       "Chronology's such a load"

——

The Cape May warbler / wormed its way
Along the elm twig dead
       No insects in that woody gray
       But still its cheek was red

slow cup

Sat down
in the Country Store
with 2-bit styro-
foam coffee
& the dark man
covered with law
enforcement badges
was saying, "I
love the flag &
Mom's apple pie
but the CIA ain't so simple."

Told how he was
eyes & ears in Laos
moving
through mountains
with mercenary
"Chinese nuns."
The "nuns" were *sanctioned*
at a certain point.

"Sanctioned?" I echoed.
"Killed," he
clarified.... "You know
those jet trails in
cowboy movies?
They're anachronisms.

Like the CIA."
He didn't say
what period the
sanctions represented.
Someone came in, waved,
called him "Bob,"
& ordered a scratch Lotto sheet.

He went on,
occasionally relieving
the punctuation of his
speech with the breath of a
laugh that didn't uncover
his upper teeth.

Through the curlicues
of slant polysyllables
he let me know
they were gonna
sanction him too
("An American!" I breathed)
so he made his way
through Burmese jungles & down
into Thailand.

But he's only got, you see,
a certain concentration
of skills.

Discretion
I hazarded
"feeds" the sophistication
internationalism
needs.

He nodded.
"The politicians
are all homosexual murderers,
& that's proof
to me
of freedom of choice."

He laughed again, breathing,
black hair neatly combed,
on his high stool
in the Country Store.

SECTION: LOOSE HAIKU & SENRYU

indefinite article

an opinion
is like a moon
in a song

PSYKU

exchange

"that was great!"

"you deserve it!"
(on the bed,
jerking about with laughter)

we *both* can't
have our cake
and eat it too

EARTH DAY — *cool Colorado* — *1993*

ant on rock
...
ragged fingernails

spit from lungs
like pupa
on soft thick light-green leaf
rosette

nature's too slow—
people get
bored

existence precedes essence
(Sartre)
& keeps on preceding it

DIDACTIKU

pepper your eggs first
then you can see
where the salt falls

inside every Messiah
is a second-hand
exploding frog joke

4 haiku from "Great Literature of the West"

it grew large
specks of dust
dancing in its whiteness
as it reached the screen

—Ralph Ellison

"Your lovely pear tree—
pear tree—
pear tree!"

—Katherine Mansfield

And he shall turn the heart of the fathers to the children
and the heart of the children to their fathers
lest I come and smite the earth with a curse

—God

In *his* time
when he was young
or even when he was only but a little less
middle-aged
the best manners had been
the best kindness
and the best kindness had mostly been
some art of not insisting
on one's luxurious differences
of concealing rather
for common humanity
if not for common decency
a part at least of the intensity
or the ferocity with which
one might be
"in the know."

—Henry James

on the Columbus Quincentenary 1992

'jever see a headline
HITLER DISCOVERS POLAND ?

why I was late for work

just drivin' thru the suburbs sippin' beer, Boss,
dreamin' about you

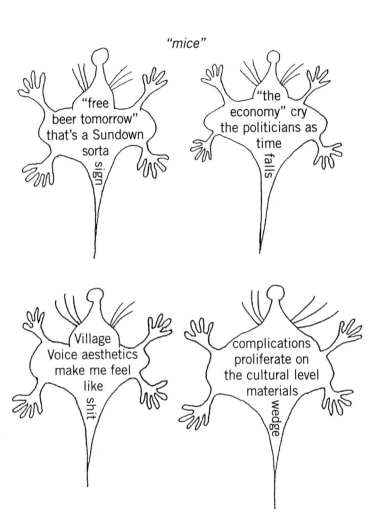

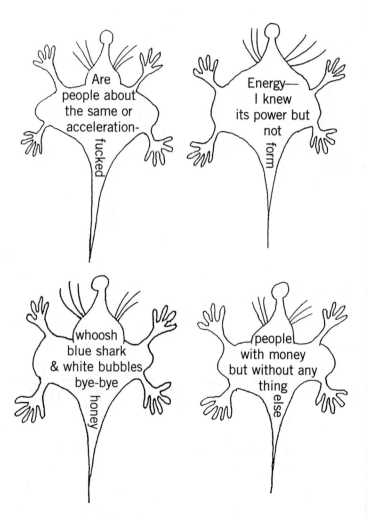

GUATE SENRYU '90

Arzú
fuma rubios
blond puffs

—

multicultural town
orange flowers
diesel smoke

—

mercado
como Safeway pero
naked & bleeding

—

everything & its dog
jumbled into climate
smooth as silk

—

no TV so
presidential candidates
paint on rocks

—

all the Quetzales
crumble
in the hand

—

Doña Beatriz
no debía bastarse
con *un* catedral negro

—

Ríos Montt
believes in basics
money & death

—

over gray jungle
screeching airplanes
the new parrots

—

corn
climbs mountains
as criollos dine

—

Cerezo
ain't no cherry
he's a banana

—

the Petén
a big salad—
& it's dinnertime!

from *SCARFACE HAIKU*

oh yeah?
what are you gonna
do about it?

—

hello, Louie
bang!
bang!

—

 yeah, I like Johnny
but I like you
more

—

 rat-a-tat-tat-tat-tat
hey
we can use those

—

 sure I'm not afraid
I'm like you, Tony
ha ha ha!

—

 don't shoot!
I got no gun!

I'm all alone...

LECTURE

Scientific tests in post-Chomskyan generative linguistics have demonstrated conclusively that beyond the splurge of consciousness we pass from a pure logic & phenomenology to physiology if we wish to maintain an equivalence between concept & remembered image, & within that shifting morphology the suprasegmental accuracy of represented metamorphosis may well be reduced via narratology by what Daniloff calls "the partially digested subjective." In lay terms, for the would-be artist:

FORGET YOURSELF. Do not take yourself seriously, *including* Ideas, no matter how achingly ultimate they seem, nor how their cloudiness turns into a Noah's Flood of clarity.

Become a beakful of mud with hands & ears & eyes, a mouth to drink coffee with, & memory. No more. It's amazing how difficult & deceptive the task of divorcing care & self is. We are all aware, with a sort of painful, gay laughter suspended in boredom, how artists inferior to or more naive than ourselves display everywhere, blatantly but unknowingly, a childish need to put themselves in a good light. Even when they're putting themselves down, they're semiconsciously crying out for adoration. It's *this* distraction that makes most art less thrilling than a dying squirrel.

We, as mature artists, feel we have transcended ego-taint in our work. But in fact the entire world-interface of *anyone* in every tiny detail is *interwoven* with piranha swarms of image need.

Children carry this like another few inches of transparent flesh. Then it sinks in, & the more adult we become the more it's part of our Very Fiber. It takes a thousand guises, emerges under masks of unvarying virtue.

"My heart reaches out to these poor people. They're figurines of Sorrow. Let's go home."

"I know a place of peace & beauty, faraway, some day."

"I adore her. That's all that matters."

These poor objects of love don't get to *exist,* except as puppets of mealy-mouthed fingers. What exists is falsified pastels of the self sloshing all available receptors.

OR: "Sittin' in the kitchen." All of *my* poems begin with these four words. & I stole *them* from my friend Richard. Too beautiful to think up. By *means* of them, I constantly wish to image forth these things, about myself:

1. I'm direct, no-nonsense.
2. I'm a keen observer ("sittin'").
3. I'm colloquial, folksy, colorful, down-home. Sittin' in the kitchen.
4. I'm economical, with words & life.
5. I'm musical.
6. I'm in tune with the warm, feminine center of things. Sittin' in the kitchen.
7. I'm humorous.
8. & I'm hungry.

Well! This winds up to be watered-down Br'er Rabbit. Desperation patches on blue hollow.—Could be worse. Art's inconvenient.

Artists have studied out positions wherein they can have a little fun with their backs to the wall; dance about with kitchen doors glued to their shoulder blades. Their whole deal is to be a step ahead of laughter, play The Fool via planned obsolescence. A total idiot, whether the condition be *natural* or gained by means of much study, as in the religions, can't *do* things, which is what artists do. That is, *things. Purity* never moves.

You might, at this point, go half-blind by feeling your face light up, not too much but just right, at the prospect of *compromise*, but that's just a bad word. Forget it. Unless it's a matter of multidimensional interexisting spheres. Unworldliness, which is what compromise leads to, is just a Gothic happy-face of zombie-white sentimentality. Black Hole of sugar. An artist has to be integral but nonrepeating, all-of-a-piece like a starfish.

Artists are like unpredictable Wall Street pirates who hack around with some genuine pigiron but protect, *inside,* this snow white egg-shaped synapse town of beautiful retardism so it's unhurt by the gorgeously cruel world & yet functions in every string of their Thing, sometimes. This is getting hard to picture, which may be because it's all wrong. It's certainly hard to *do*. Artists whine a lot, but they seek novel whines.

You really need a 3-D computer screen for this, & that's why nobody ever digs the graphics well enough to get a further insight. Meanwhile, this tender, icy synapse-egg is maintained, in terms of ordinary hydraulics, & functions like a thermostat. Its humanoid shell is both more & less human than the average, depending on what "human" means.

All language emits the metallic stench of statement. The statement is invariably the person of the statement-maker. So you might as well just start playing around, & *play hard*. This is nobility.

Charity is a cheap shot. It's as if by throwing 86 cents on the ground you have a brick. Or by saying "Brick" you become one. The magic of names is much more expensive. You may become electrically connected to a brick by forgetting the name. You may become electrically connected to a poem by keeping the name & forgetting what it means. You may pick up a brick & throw it. At me. I *need* the attention. But *don't worry*, because all these insights are perfectly sound.

These insights are boiled in a selfless hot ether, paintakingly plucked from the wisdom surrounding decades of sincerity, & dressed in a clever motley.

I have a dream.

I mean, y'know what I mean? I mean, I've been making choices here, forsaking my food and exercise, on the basis of a perfect crystal of goodness, which you didn't realize. But now it's time to reveal this as a personal essay. But *don't* worry, I *know* what I'm doing. *Don't worry*. It's not that I can't practice what I preach & forget myself. I *can*. I just don't *want* to right now, because I'm willing to sacrifice *my* dignity for *your* edification, & besides I have another, perfect dignity just below the one I'm tossing away now.

Actually, what I'm doing, in a sense, is cunningly bucking the tide of your latest perception of the intentional fallacy's borders by jumping *right into it.* Know what I mean? Like, the intentional fallacy's where sincerity makes liars of us all. *You* know, declaration runs us stone-blind. But if you just turn around & get *double* sincere, then you *fool* the system because you use something that got blocked off, which is good (sincerity, y'know), but you're outside *too* so you don't partake of its preachy crap. It's kinda like the camp appreciation of "White Christmas" jingling back into a yellow haze. So, anyway, that's what I'm doing.

Sure, I'm not the first, I'm just *in* the breeze. Opposites are alike, uh-huh, but it's the twist of the knife that cuts the mustard. I *really* know what I'm doing. But *doesn't* this make you just a trifle nauseous? When I *say* that? Sure, & I *know* that. That's what I'm *doing.* & the way I stay on top of your nausea is this: by *telling* you about it! I *know* what you're thinking. Like sticking the bridal pair on top of the wedding cake. What can you *do* (don't tell me)? Like, chattering like an idiot savant in the five-&-dime. Stupidity has its beauty (which gets old because it's so damn eternal), but when you get into *off*-stupid, like falling off a rope, you're approaching *sub*-stupid. A*ha,* the alpha state. Right? But when I *tell* you this, I mean, it falls right into Ezra Pound, &, y'know, rhythm can go *any*where. The whole purpose is to get into what you know. Basic chatter.

Let's take a breath. An attractive version of knowledge, poetically now, would be in the field of ranching tips, or community finance. *Textural acts* as beautiful as cellular fission, slicing then from now. But all these varieties of barbwire fence & Brooklyn Dodger candy bars are attempts to *paint yourself up* so as to resemble the off-white solidity of a hospital bed. Yes. I wanna cut *right through* that. I was *born,* & I'm twice-divorced but it wasn't my *fault.* In fact, in the last analysis, these divorces were all a beautiful adventure. I've actually extracted gristle, from fake wood, in a living graph that whispers "beautiful adventure," like a telephone line to your dream's bathroom, because I'm a bloody beautiful guy. My hand would be steadier castrating a pig, but that, & the breakfast afterwards, & the old beige farmhouse, are all categorized by now. *True* truth lies in what's ordinarily swept under the bridge & called "pettiness," really curved light when you just take a minute of your time & look at it.

So, articulation never builds its own floor. You might as well give that up. I mean, history is nice if you just want to be a sideshow type like Metternich.—But let me tell you some more about myself.

I'm idealistic in a sort of golden way that I cherish because of its sheer nobility, but I'm also vividly colorful & as realistic as a brown bear, in a *very* attractive total melange. I understand everything. The fact that I haven't attracted an unruly cadre of slavish cognoscenti, or even *one fan,* is simply due to the fact that I'm ultra-subtle &

ahead of my time, & I pad beautiful lost trails in my lone-wolf sorta way.

I'm also very youthful & vigorous, basically, but at the same time old & wise, not to mention "in the middle," which is very balanced & *good.* I'm even sorta crippled & not crippled, like Lord Byron, depending on my mood. I mean, it's *totally* real, & I can back it up, but if you were to ask me about it, which nobody ever does, I'd answer in a kindly but objective manner which certainly wouldn't exceed 3 or 4 hours, include some medical terms. I've been very heroic about it & I *never* speak of it, because all I care about is positive things. It's *very* interesting though. Also I'd like to mention frankly that I'm good in bed, take my word for it, I'm referring to *fucking* y'know—at least I used to be before being melodramatically "mugged" by my tragic illness, which had nothing to do with drinking. *Nothing* goes to my head. My shit has a rather pleasant farm aroma.

Don't misunderstand me & crowd around wanting to touch me & suck my brains, I *really* don't have much time, but that's all *part* of it. Y'know I have a lot of courage, y'know, to stand up here & talk like a Beautiful Fool (but not the *specious* kind) so you all can learn to find happiness in your lives.

Am I happy myself? Oh yes, yet in a way that *includes* deeply post-up-to-date gut sorrow.

However, my delicate sense of modesty, resembling in many ways the italianate shapeliness of ultimate light & shadow, draws me away from this frank discussion.

Back to *art,* not that this only *seeming* digression was-
n't, in its blend (but *not* blend in the *homogeneous*
sense) of outrage & buried eu*clid*ishness, a vegetarian
spaceship looking down on the postmodern. It was.

. Art, it has been amply demonstrated, is the justifica-
tion, in flipped hindsight, of civilization. Might as well try
it. It's almost as pretty as everything else. Now. You're
gonna have ego "problems." So just *deny* them! Present-
day psychology has amassed just enough knowledge that
its recommendations are all ass-backwards. It's like the
discovery of pus.— Oh wow, it's real, let's turn the whole
body into this stuff! Forget that. They're at that *stage*
where you act free by *precepts*, the quivering light-green
edge of age 13. The only thing that saves hipness is the
breathtaking beauty of its lies. Here are my recommendations. Let your need to wallow in self-pity *(which* is just
another chemical) emerge in convoluted petty ways that
really make people work to halfway pigeonhole because
they're so simple. *That's it!* You lay eggs on people's hands
while they're holding on to something. Simplicity *itches* to
become complex. I *could* just spit on the floor & tell you
about geranium seeds &/or artificial colors but you're
probably not ready for that. You've got a wire through your
throat. *Nothing* is what we think it is: a big zilch. Can't tell
where it's coming from. Take my "word" for it.

So back to forgetting self in art, you realize of course
that my *apparent* trumpeting of self is in fact a *real
trumpet,* golden brass & spit & bell-motion, much more
self-transcendent than the pretensions of Objectivism,

since I *knowingly* cast myself into the perspective of a *whiff* of comic figure, which in turn is *pure atoms.*

Forget yourself in art. Exceptions prove the rule because they're like weird faces that pop & swirl up when you're not looking. You may think you know this, but it's *dumb* of you to think like that. I've discovered that to be so, like a diamond. I discovered it in Western Springs, Illinois, on a roller-coaster hall of mirrors, the *very first day.* I was the center of the universe then, thinking about sex with a package of hot dogs. Going Hey bop a lula boppa spiffety bam dee bop a lula bop a libbidy-do.

Thank you.

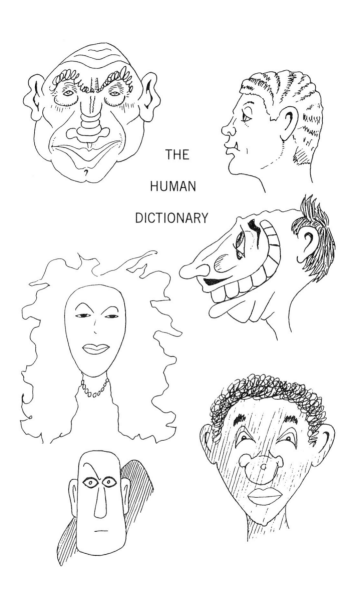

THE

HUMAN

DICTIONARY

(EXCERPT)

ASSOCIATED DEFINITIONS

civilized: Out of hand.

civilization: The accretion of gratuitous acts forming an opaque shield.

art: The attempt to recreate life within civilization (see above).

culture: The loss of perspective.

music: A fancy clock.

dance: Attempt to aesthetically justify bipedalism.

theater: A focus at a comfortable distance.

poetry: The hubris of believing a gray code could resemble life.

fiction: A drug with no physical side-effects but bed-sores.

painting: An obscure 2-D smear habit which caters to the simplistic image-construct capability of human memory.

sculpture: Geological travesty.

architecture: A bull in a bird's nest.

"far-sightedness": In chronology, as used, analogous to the ability spatially to barely locate the end of your nose.

human knowledge: a fractional sifting of information in the first place, further severely reduced by organic limits, the pitiful remainder grotesquely distorted by mind needing to fit all input into minuscule comfort zone, & to paint over & mis-shape & eviscerate it; this unsavory dregs cut & falsified more yet towards its representation in the short-armed shorthand of language—then censored, blotted, bleached, spayed, & twisted even further for mass consumption—so that we may claim to know something. The result is like a few specks crumbled from a dry turd, stuck to a funhouse mirror, being smugly hailed as "dog!" by carnival crowds.

human wisdom: Possible shapeliness of a handful of dust.

human philosophy: Wrinkles in a vacuum.

human education: the broadening of ignorance.

human love: Slow eating.

human eschatology: a tautological pleonasm.

humane: A word, like "shoppe," wherein ornament can't conceal the basic tawdriness.

male human: Sperm ejector with pretensions.

female human: Basic fact yearning to be a hallucination.

white human: A bubble on the soup.

black human: Squeaky wheel drowned in grease.

business human: Pimp, time-bomb salesman.

political human: Believer that truth is *relative*—like a rotten uncle he's got the goods on.

young human: Baby with big muscles & cavernous needs.

old human: Porcelain smile surmounting pain—finally at rest after a lifetime of strenuous pollution.

SECTION: ECO-ACROSTICS

in the

B asement, my father put
A cage, & a rabbit. Bye & bye
B abies were born. "They are
Y ours," my parents said. The babies

R olled
A round on chickenwire
B ecause I was too panicked to
B ring paper & all the things they needed. They died.
I t was a horror. A number of dead babies scattered there on wire.
T hat's a little
S tory of the world.

D eclares that life without buffers of miscellany
I sn't
R eal but an incomplete
T hought.

"H ey!" we said, hearing the cries, "there's
 A redtail nest in Salt Creek
W oods." Spotted it in a hickory. She
K ept circling, screaming, & I
S hinnied up,

N earing her home... SLAM! Hard-in-the-back!
 E xcalibur (hawk's-fist)!—whirlaway feathers—grab hold (tree)—
 S un spins in leaves—down the trunk I slide. & away; I could see
 T hat hard-handed mama hawk out-essenced me.

crystal

Nuzzle
Arch
Trot
Unite
Ramify
Erase.

Nothing
At all's outside
This total
Universe, yet it
Raditates
Essentials.

Net
Aggregate
Truth
Unties
Regular
Experience.

Not
All
Time's
Under
Relativity's
Example.

Nerves
Actuate
That
Utterly
Rolling
Elegance.

No one's
At home!
The
Ugly
Reality's
Evanescence.

ecology 101

W ord
O f
R elated
L ife &
D eath.

C ontrol
O ver
R eality's
P retense.

O rganizing
R esources
A ccording
T o money
I s
O rderly
N egation of
S oul & body.

man with a plan

G ive
E ternity a
N anosecond,
E arthwise—
'T will
I nsist on
C omplete
S pace.

futures

P rophecy
R olls
O n.
"F ree enterprise skids on an
I nch of
T ime.

Collom

free meter

OK, so a really unexpected miracle happened in '95,
Suddenly, it seemed, the voice(s) of reason prevailed
& the human world, as one, began to act as if being alive
With such powers took planning. Had catastrophe failed?

Everyone joined in reduction of reproduction.
Earth's population shrank, a fraction of the prior
Figure; habits, too, were moderated, & the suction
Of topsoil waned, reversed. Goodness like a prairie fire

Spread across the globe.
                         A few hundred years passed
& people became restive. What the fuck, they thought,
All that 20th-Century piss & vinegar turned out harmless at
last —
We can stop like they did; there's no such thing as "ought."

So they resumed building lots of fun machines & grabbing
power,
But this time,
              you know how it goes,
                                    skidded into the
                                              final hour.

1-15-95

robins

I've never heard the robins squabble-squall
So much; I've never seen so many pressed
In a single patio before. I suppose that all
Of us (people) are prone to "burst the nest"

(To twist the trope) and cause a bloody ruckus.
Outside *our* fragile ball of mud and sticks,
Howe'er, there ain't no more material, so fuck us.
We'll let The World float down the River Styx.

And now: sestet. Ahem. The planet Frank-
Enstein awaits us in the fifth dimension.
Hey! No sweat, we'll cry all the way to the bank.
Dead stuff from space—no need for any tension.

Well, glad to've quenched fear with these cheerful
words.
Amazing wisdom wells from watching birds.

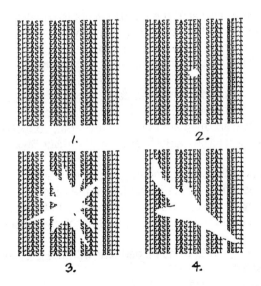

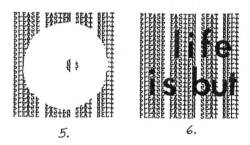

5.

6.

A DREA ▪

7.

8.

ecology

SURROUNDED BY BONE, SURROUNDED BY CELLS,
BY RINGS, BY RINGS OF HELL, BY HAIR, SURROUNDED BY
AIR-IS-A-THING, SURROUNDED BY SILHOUETTE, BY
    HONEY WET BEES, YET
BY SKELETONS OF TREES, SURROUNDED BY ACTUAL,
    YES, FOR PRACTICAL
PURPOSES, PEOPLE, SURROUNDED BY SURREAL
POPCORN, SURROUNDED BY THE REBORN: SURRENDER
    IN THE CENTER
TO SURROUNDINGS. O SURRENDER FOREVER, NEVER
END HER, LET HER BLEND AROUND, SURRENDER TO
    SURROUNDINGS THAT
SURROUND THE TENDER ENDO-SURRENDER, THAT
TUMBLE THROUGH THE TUMBLING TO THAT BLUE THAT
CURLS AROUND THE CRUMBLING, TO THAT, THE BLUE THAT
RUMBLES UNDER THE SUN BOUNDING THE PEARL THAT
WE WALK ON, TALK ON; WE CAN CHALK THAT
UP TO EXPERIENCE, SENSING THE BROWN HERE THAT'S
BLUE NOW, A DROP OF WATER SURROUNDING A COW
    THAT'S
BLACK & WHITE, THE WARBLING BLACKBURNIAN TWIT-
    TER THAT'S
MACHINING MIDNIGHT ORANGE IN THE LIGHT THAT'S
GLITTERING IN THE LIGHT GREEN VISIBLE WIND. THAT'S
THE TICKET TO THE TUNNEL THROUGH THE THICKET
    THAT'S
A CRICKET'S FUNNEL OF MUSIC TO CORRECT & PICK IT OUT
FROM UNDER THE WING THAT WHIRLS UP OVER & OUT!

NIGHTMARE TURQUOISE VIII

E cology of disappearance (since
N o end's in sight). The *word* descries a blind
V ariety, 'round point too white to mince;
I n *ding an sich,* the thing is hard to find.

R enewal needs a prime rapport with time,
O r all the dots of "true" will be but dark-
N ess, Plato's Park, just memory to mime:
M nemosyne pushed up a tree, her bark

E xtracted rhyme. The basic sound of tree
N o ground alone can sing, for (knock on wild)
T he crux is in the structure; sky to sea
A nd rock to soil, it's style delivers child.

L et's love in time, recoup the primal soup,
I mpell all "group" to *symbiotic loop.*

Ecology
Of disappea-
Rance (since no end's in
     sight).
The *word* descries
a blind vari-
Ety, 'round point too white

To mince; in *ding*
An sich, the thing
Is hard to find. Renew-

Al needs a prime
Rapport with time,
Or all the dots of "true"

Will be but dark-
Ness, Plato's Park, just
Memory to mime:

Mnemosyne
Pushed up a tree,
Her bark extracted rhyme.

The basic sound
Of tree no ground
Alone can sing, for (knock

On wild) the crux
Is in the struc-
Ture; sky to sea & rock

To soil, it's style
Delivers child.
L et's love in time, recoup

The primal soup,
Impell all "group"
to *symbiotic loop.*

LUCUBRATION

A Verse History of a Scandal

Just a half century after our liberation
From Anglification
Without representation
Came the initiation
Of a nice bit of democratization
Here, a type of money concentration
Named savings-&-loans but affectionately called "thrifts"
     because they represented the implementation
Of a prudent instinct in the laboring classes—*plus* their
     realization
Via low-interest mortgages of the power to purchase
     modest homes.
     A clarification
Was built in that there couldn't be a sudden negation
Of some little guy's or gal's life savings by means of
     any irresponsible management monetary pavanne
     or divagation.
The institutions traded freedom for the promise of
     emergency inhalation
Of federal funds in case of an untoward indentation
Of their assets. This all especially gelled under FDR, &,
     with interest rates in a happy state of petrification
Up into the 1960's, seemed a fairly hunky-dory amelio-
     ration
Of Depression, World War, automation,
And other glitches of modernization.
Then Lyndon, who after all had but one unhealthy life-
     time in which to garner total glorification,

Pushed a glorious land war against the commie Asian
Hordes and at the same time printed *lots of money* for
the vivification
Of the domestic situation.
Result, inflation.
He and Dicky pulled paper *off* the mineral, relative
unshakability of gold so it started blowing in the
wind—fluctuation.
And the A-rabs suddenly decided oil was indeed the
lifeblood of industrialization;
They began *charging* for it, to everyone else's lamenta-
tion.
And Volker's Federal Reserve quelled the indiscrimi-
nate masturbation
Of green paper—voila! instant interest elevation.
The thrifts were suddenly suffering frustration
Since they weren't allowed to pay high *deposit* interest,
which caused everybody to "lose interest" and run
to the money markets with uninsured elation.
And, on the other side of the ledger, the thrifts could-
n't charge high *loan* interest—not on the white-
picket-fence-with-a-few-roses-curling-up-it homes
of this folksily puissant nation.
Well, round about now we're up to 1980 and, lo,
Reaganization.
Money problems looming? Gosh, good golfing men who
play with money represent our very foundation;
We'll turn 'em loose and soon resolve any perturbation
(Though, like enough, the reported indication
Is just some lefty defecation,
The, gulp, dysentery of too much education).

So as a literal after-thought in a late-night session
    Congressionals let the thrifts pay more on deposits
    (so they could lose a little on each one but make it
    up in volume-ization)
And, at the same time, raised the then $40,000 feder-
    al coverage for each depositor to $100,000—a
    great golden chug-a-lug libation.
Since the rule stating only 5% of a thrift's deposits
    could be brokered had undergone a silent cessation,
And you know how wonderful communication
Has become, *daily* nationwide searches for the highest
    deposit interest rate grew keen with systemization,
And the thrifts, seeking deposits like quivering vaults
    of ovulation,
Lost any vestige of moderation,
Found themselves full of high-cost venture capitalization.
Don Regan loved this stuff—Merrill Lynch was a verita-
    ble annexation
Of S&L desire for any & all fiduciary pustulation.
By 1982 the "industry" was as broke as a rowboat
    Haitian,
But the lobbyist myrmidons, via Freddy St. Germain,
    Chairman of the House Banking Committee,
    blocked the necessary mild purgation
And fixed things by *halving* the percentage-of-assets
    real-money requirement, so all a thrift needed to
    have on hand now was a cupful of coins and a
    cockful of imagination.
Presto, they *looked* as healthy as Percheron ejaculation,
And even more so when Accounting Practices had such
    "modification"

Performed on it there was no such thing as a violation

Any more. So papers *shone* with handsome profits while
the last actual lucrative lactation

Was dribbling down the drain like some forlorn
reformer's allegation.

And they cut out the lotsa-little-guys ownership rule so
anyone with a big-bux fixation

Could run things *sans* fear of that bothersome vexation,

Consultation,

Common to any democratic organization.

The new, lone owner didn't even need purchase cash,
just a relation-

Ship with some pal who'd appraise his, say, acre of lost
sagebrush as a future-settlement sensation.

And the thrifts were allowed to lend without a down pay-
ment, to anyone, in any location,

For any dubious exploration.

No more simple amortization

Of Mr. & Mrs. Jones's five-room. Then the *state* thrifts,
which had long been happy trading campaign
donation

For local regulatory liberalization,

Either jumped to the feds or, in rapid Californication,

Started tossing "their" money into everything from
corporation

Piracy to Martian gold mines to perpetual-motion
machination.

Good old boys would sit around flipping some flat dusty
chunk of tarnation

Twenty times a night, picking up loan fees at every
revelation,

I mean revolution. When a buddy-loan was due, there
    wasn't no expectation,
Just *another* loan to cover, another striation
In a sweet layer-cake so thick it was an immunization
Against investigation.

Sometimes they'd slop up a mock run of buildings for
    the edificecation
Of any regulator not entirely under sedation,
And park junked cars by 'em, to serve visualization
Of Progress & Application,
Or, Texas civilization.
And if by some chance that didn't seem sufficient
    suffocation
Of appearances, they'd pack everything with such a
    paperous complication
Of "daisy chains," fake subsidiaries, & assorted documents
    as to make a law library look like a simplification.
Even beyond all this amplification
Lay the simple pocket-plop of salarization.
Not to mention the lovely loyalty effect of subordinate
    subsidization
And the financial concentration
Available through nepotation.
And then they'd mad-money up some private air forces,
    etc., for incidental recreation.

Not even millions of years of meditation
By a massive delegation
Of the sharpest mathematicians in creation
Could ever tell us where all those billions took a vacation.

Once Lamar S&L of Texas applied to open a branch on
    the moon—true lunarization
Of greed. By the mid-80's even such an item of regular
    Reaganite pullulation
As Ed Gray, if he carried a kernel of courage, could see
    it was all a giant aberration,
The willful hallucination
Attendant on our dollar-sign coronation.
When he showed Don Regan evidence of conspicuous
    consummation
To the point of satiation,
Regan grinned through his caviar, thought it devoutly
    to be wished, took it as a certification
Of the salubrious regeneration
Of American intensification
Of Enterprise possible via deregulation.
David Stockman of White House OMB made the
    determination
Of pay & numbers investigators; thus turnover,
    fragmentation,
And lack of job qualification,
Plus intimidation,
Knocked out any installation
Much less continuation
Of skills in regulation.
Any supplication
For congressional redress was about as effective as
    expectoration
Into a conflagation.
In fact, a congregation
Of Senators DeConcini, McCain, Cranston, Glenn, and

Riegle dealt Gray some verbal excoriation
For causing poor Keating, the Mephistophelean yup
    who'd plied their coffers with monetary animation,
Undue excruciation,
Wanted Gray's resignation.
Jim Wright spewed & respewed a similar peroration.
Things were too far gone for any reparation
By "good business," so a quietude as of pure
    vegetation
Settled over the scene. With fascination
One could watch Dukakis, if one knew, utterly avoid
    one iota of information-
AI instigation,
Since a bunch of his buds were buried in it to the
    point of solidification.
And the election—and the delectation
Of the new Prez, with earnest intonation,
Paternal frowns, and a dewy carnation,
Delivering, as a fresh divination,
This S&L as-it-were Blip of uglification.
He'd appearently just clambered out of a decade's
    hibernation
In time for his finger-wagging pontification.
What a Bushwhackization,
And inside-out sanctification,
With Little Neil scrambling for crumbs of purification.

And now, the pacification,
In the course of which embarkation
Using ancient Resolution Trust bonds for deceptive
    pigmentation

The configuration
Of our loss will swell & swell like a drunken explanation.
One seventieth (even of existing fraud referrals) are
    scheduled for litigation.
There's no design against a coming ruination
Of commercial banks and/or insurance. No expiation.
No renunciation.
No real emendation.
Little incarceration,
Some probation.
But *lots* of taxation,
And more taxation to pursue the running equation
Of time and growing interest, & more taxation yet, for
    the lubrication
And reintegration
Of all that wasteland flipped & reflipped without
    hesitation.
More sweetheart desert deals than spots on a
    Dalmatian.

And the "taxation" of reconciliation
To a quickened elimination.

Sonnet

NATURE...

Means anything but "sense" but penetrates
Your little nutshell. Terms of light recover
Everything that eye or star creates;
You have to know the loving from the lover.

Romantic copies classicize the brain.
A speck becomes a color, as the point
Of light first found became a round refrain,
A layered thing that darkness may anoint.

You break an egg. And fantasy flies across
The field, black gold and silver, and another
Vision cracks; one cell contains no loss
But shine and shadow. Spectra make it mother:

Sacrifice chiaroscuro *in* you,
Till gestures of the mind alone continue.

SCIENCE NEWS

Does nonsense DNA speak its own dialect   November 10, 1994

When geneticists first began to
decipher the DNA code, they naturally
focused on genes. That's where the
action is, they thought. After all,
genes specify the amino acids that make
up proteins, the molecules required for
life.

That focus neglects some 90 per-
cent of the DNA in a cell.

DNA exists the cell nucleus as long
strands paired nuc leotides, o5 base pairs.
Genes occupy particular of these DNA
strands called chromosomes. In gene,
each set three nucleotides "spells" a particulare
aminoacid. Taken together, these sets
code for very particular protein.

Stretches seemingly meaningless DNA
separate. Gibberish also lie between coded within geen. Long ignored "junk," noncoding DNA
nevert-
heless its own Michael SimOns, a molecular
at Harvard School in Boston. He his c
colleagues working Rsoatio N. Mantegna
and other Boston University languagelike
properties in this junk junk junk.

Applied two to from of simp
le and
complex 437 at least 50,000 base as as
shorter one 2.2 million? possible and
noncoding .

Boston
one mistake
explains
Boston
in of
can still be

Also, the frequency with which var—
ous three-, four-, five-, six-, seven-, and
eight-based pair patterns appear in non-
just
the group reports

10,000
10th
1,0000
100, Stanley explains

Collom

recognizze

unfamiliar
Andrzej K. Konopka
nonprofit

structured
peo ple

some
   close
    regionss
    whair
break
        translaite
        Stanley

                              Indeed

                    need

         really does

                              but that

              this

              no

                        Goldberger

      force.
                we

A Few Remarks at Little Red Rocks

my feet almost in the ditch
water-striders work fulltime
just to stay here
thistle, grama grass, three-awn, mountain mahogany
crowd the waterside
artemisia's got more room
on the uphill side, next to a big pink rock
below a couple ponderosa
squall of Steller's jay &
the big red rocks might serve
with their scalloped edges
as stepping stones to the clouds
but the color scheme goes crazy—blue & white
suddenly sunlight intensifies
from behind me
& a tiny bug, god knows what
runs over this yellow paper

NOTHING IS SO BEAUTIFUL AS NOTHING IS SO BEAUTIFUL AS NOTHING IS

Found Object

The terrible famine and accompanying disease
which caused the death
of over a thousand people on St. Lawrence Island
during the winter of 1879
and 1880 was said to have
been caused by the use of whiskey.
The people of that island usually
obtained their supply of food
for the winter by
killing walrus from the great herds of these animals
that go through Bering strait
on the first ice in the fall.
The walrus remain about the island
only a few days
and then go south, when
the ice closes about
and shuts the island in
till spring.

Just before the time for the walrus
to reach the island
that season, the Eskimo obtained a supply
of whiskey from some vessels
and began a prolonged debauch,
which ended only
when the supply was exhausted.
When this occurred the
annual migration of the walrus had passed, and the

people were shut in for the
winter
by
the ice.
The result was that over two-thirds of the population
died before
spring. The
following spring, when the *Corwin*
visited the islands,
some of the survivors came
on board bringing a few articles for trade.
They wished only to purchase
rifle cartridges and more whiskey.

During July, 1881,
the *Corwin* made a visit to this famine-stricken district,
where the miserable survivors were seen.
Only a single dog
was left among them,
the others
having been eaten by the starving people.
Two of the largest villages were
entirely depopulated.

On the bluff
at the northwest point of this island
we found a couple of surviving families living in round-
top, walrus hide
summer houses.
The adults seemed very much depressed.
Among them were two

bright little girls.
When I shot a snow bunting near the village
they called to me
and ran to show me its nest
on the hillside.

When I asked
one of the inhabitants what had become
of the people who formerly lived
on that part of the island, he
waved his hand toward the winter village,
saying, "All *mucky mucky*,"
being the jargon term for "dead."

I tried to obtain a photograph of the women and little girls,
and for that purpose
placed them in position and focused the camera.
While I was waiting for a lull in the wind
to take the picture,
the husband of one of the women came up
and asked in a listless, matter-of-fact tone, "All *mucky* now?"
meaning, "Will they all die now?"
He evidently took it for granted
that my camera was a conjuring box,
which would complete the work of the
famine, yet he seemed perfectly
indifferent to
the consequences.

> (from *The Eskimo About Bering Strait,*
> Edward William Nelson,
> Government Printing Office, 1900)

rhythm

people only want you to surprise them certain ways

end

Anselm Hollo, born in Finland and settling in the United States in 1966, is a poet, literary translator, and on the Core Faculty of the Jack Kerouac School of Disembodied Poetics at The Naropa Institute. His numerous books include *No Complaints, Pick Up The House, Outlying Districts, And How On Earth, Corvus* and the translation *Hipponax of Ephesus*. He is the recent recipient of a distinguished translator's award from the Finnish Arts Council.

Anne Waldman founded the Jack Kerouac School of Disembodied Poetics with Allen Ginsberg in 1974, after serving as the Director of The Poetry Project at St. Mark's Church In-the-Bowery in New York City for over a decade. She is the author, most recently, of the epic poem *IOVIS* (Books I & II), *Kill or Cure* and co-translator of *Songs of The Sons and Daughters of Buddha* (with Andrew Schelling). She is also editor of *The Beat Book* and recipient of the Shelley Memorial Award for poetry in 1996. She is a celebrated performer of her own work.

Jack Collom teaches ecology-poetics and oversees Project Outreach at The Jack Kerouac School of Disembodied Poetics where he has been resident faculty for over a decade. A prolific writer, he has been published in over a hundred magazines and anthologies in the USA and abroad. His books include *Arguing With Something Plato Said, The Task* and *Entering The City*. He has worked extensively with the Teachers and Writers Collaborative in New York City and published his *ars poetica* on teaching poetry, *Moving Windows*, under their aegis.

AUTONOMEDIA BOOK SERIES

Jim Fleming, Editor

SEMIOTEXT(E) NATIVE AGENTS SERIES
Chris Kraus, Editor

SEMIOTEXT(E) FOREIGN AGENTS SERIES
Jim Fleming & Sylvère Lotringer, Editors

PLOVER PRESS

THE COURAGE TO STAND ALONE
U. G. Krishnamurti

THE MOTHER OF GOD
Luna Tarlo

AUTONOMEDIA DISTRIBUTION

DRUNKEN BOAT
An Anarchist Review of Literature & the Arts
Max Blechman, ed.

LUSITANIA
A Journal of Reflection & Oceanography
Martim Avillez, ed.

FELIX
The Review of Television & Video Culture
Kathy High, ed.

RACE TRAITOR
A Journal of the New Abolitionism
John Garvey & Noel Ignatiev, eds.

XXX FRUIT
Anne D'Adesky, ed.

BENEATH THE EMPIRE OF THE BIRDS
Carl Watson

LIVING IN VOLKSWAGEN BUSES
Julian Beck

I SHOT MUSSOLINI
Elden Garnet

ANARCHY AFTER LEFTISM
Bob Black

ALL COTTON BRIEFS
M. Kasper

PAGAN OPERETTA
Carl Honcock Rux

SKULL HEAD SAMBA
Eve Packer

BROKEN NOSES & METEMPSYCHOSES
Michael Carter

WATERWORN
Star Black

DIGITAS
New York Digital Review of Arts & Literature

AUTONOMEDIA CALENDARS

AUTONOMEDIA CALENDAR
OF JUBILEE SAINTS
Radical Heroes for the Millennium
James Koehnline & Autonomedia Collective

SHEROES &
WOMYN WARRIORS CALENDAR
Great Revolutionary Womyn of Herstory
*O.R.S.S.A.S.M. (Organisation of
Revolutionary Socialist Sisters and Some Men)*

SEMIOTEXT(E) DOUBLE AGENTS SERIES
Jim Fleming & Sylvère Lotringer, Editors

FATAL STRATEGIES
Jean Baudrillard

FOUCAULT LIVE
Collected Interviews of Michel Foucault
Sylvère Lotringer, ed.

ARCHEOLOGY OF VIOLENCE
Pierre Clastres

LOST DIMENSION
Paul Virilio

AESTHETICS OF DISAPPEARANCE
Paul Virilio

BURROUGHS LIVE
Collected Interviews of William S. Burroughs
Sylvère Lotringer, ed.